THE MONUMENTAL ERA

THE MONUMENTAL ERA

EUROPEAN ARCHITECTURE AND DESIGN
1929–1939

FRANCO BORSI

RIZZOLI NEW YORK

First published in the United States of America in 1987 by
RIZZOLI INTERNATIONAL PUBLICATIONS, INC.
597 Fifth Avenue, New York, NY 10017

Copyright © 1986 Hazan, Paris
English translation © 1987
Lund Humphries Publishers Ltd, London/
Rizzoli International Publications Inc, New York

ISBN 0-8478-0805-X
LC   87-45386

Translated by Pamela Marwood

Printed and bound in West Germany

ACKNOWLEDGEMENTS

We are grateful to the following for their co-operation in the preparation of this work: Jean-Louis Cohen, Florence Courte (Nouveau Musée, Villeurbanne), Françoise Delaporte (Musée des Arts décoratifs), Claude Ferrero, Madame Froidevaux, Guys van Hensbergen, Annie Jacques, Anatole Kopp, Conway Lloyd Morgan, Professor Luciano Patetta, Professor Joachim Petsch, Pierre Plattier, Sylvie Raulet, Madame Sarrabezolles, Vittorio Savi, Helsene Timsit, Marion Tournon-Branley and Anne van Loo.

We also thank the following galleries in Paris: Vallois (41 rue de Seine), Marcilhac (8 rue Bonaparte), Couvrat-Desvergnes (12 rue Guénégaud); and also Jose Alvarez of Editions du Regard, and the company Van Cleef et Arpels.

CONTENTS

Introduction   9

'Eupalinos ou l'architecte'   16

Architecture and revolution   22
    Fascist Italy – Nazi Germany – Communist Russia

The monumental order   52
    Classicism – Gothic – Cubism –
    Volumes – Surfaces – Proportion

National spirit   94
    England – Germany and Austria – Italy –
    Belgium – Holland – Scandinavia – France

Materials   175

Conclusion – Perspectives   193

Notes   198

Selected bibliography   201

List of illustrations   203

Photocredits   204

Index   205

INTRODUCTION

Half a century now separates us from the decade of the 1930s. Sufficient time should have elapsed for us to see that period in historical perspective, with the dialectic points blunted, the ideological clashes able to be viewed objectively, the white heat of emotions tempered by reflection, the factious arguments elucidated. Nothing is less true, however, of the decade leading up to the Second World War, from the Wall Street Crash in September 1929, to Hitler's invasion of Poland in September 1939. Throughout those ten years there was a kind of cultural decadence evident in Western Europe, which it is still hard for even the professional historian to analyse. Puzzling factors remain which are not to be explained simply as a longing for the past. After the high season of the Art Nouveau revival, art galleries still expressed such a longing by displaying furniture and *objets d'art* evocative of that period; fashion had already exploited it to the full and was busy finding other fields to revisit and reinterpret.

Architecture, by contrast, was dedicated in a single-minded way to the establishment of the so-called Modern Movement, and while not exactly rejecting the products of 1930s architecture and decorative arts as academic, reactionary and conservative, it remained uninspired by them. But facile summaries do little to help, and the puzzles remain. One is the question as to why the Classicism of the dictatorships, both Fascist and Nazi, should in the same period have been the architectural language in the democracies of Europe and America too, and also in Soviet Russia, that land which had first fired the hopes of the avant-garde and then become a bitter legend for the left-wing intelligentsia of Europe. Puzzling too are the reasons for the 'return to order', accompanied by a decline in influence of the avant-garde, and the questionable formation of a true 1930s style, identifiable as 'Novecento'[1], a style that combined formal characteristics and features in the same way as the styles which preceded it – Art Nouveau and Art Deco. It should be pointed out at once that after the relative coherence of Art Deco, Novecento presented a more complex dialectic between tradition and modernity, in that it incorporated influences from the second wave of Futurism as well as links with the past and tradition. The Novecento style, which is inseparable from a critique of the 1930s, did not in fact last very long and the reason is precisely that it did not elaborate a really coherent and easily identifiable system of signs, nor did it catch on rapidly in the same way as Art Nouveau and Art Deco.

What we can still find in the contradictions inherent in Novecento is the dialectic between ancient and modern, avant-garde and retrospective, ideology and formalism, which in the end forms the basis for the present-day conflict between modern and post-modern.

The decade of the 1930s opened with an economic depression that swallowed up as much wealth as the First World War, that accentuated social contrasts, plunged into crisis not only the capitalist economy but the very notion of liberty itself, led to new responsibilities and duties on the part of the State, and made people look with interest and sometimes with sympathy (or at least indulgence) on the attempts to resolve the conflict between Liberalism and Socialism by means of Fascist corporatism and National Socialism. Europe in the 1930s saw dictatorships spring up even on its periphery such as in Portugal and Greece, while in the middle of the decade there erupted the tragedy of the Spanish Civil War. Dictatorship as order, and aspirations towards durability, continuity and national identity were virtually mocked by the Treaty of Versailles, and ineffectively backed by the League of Nations.

In architecture, the decade actually began with the competition for the League of Nations building in Geneva, the results of which saw the establishment of the monumental order under the presidency of Victor Horta, known as 'Baron Horta', the leading figure in the Belgian Art Nouveau movement. Aesthetic aspirations reflected those in the socio-political field. Calls to order had already been heard; Cocteau had written his *Rappel à l'ordre* in 1926, and Le Corbusier had uttered his *trois rappels* in *Vers une architecture*, the second edition of which appeared in 1924. Call or return to order (the signs had been obvious for some time, and in a certain sense the First World War can be considered as a 'restoration') – the term implies a universal phenomenon which in reality it was not, and suggests that critical opinion was a kind of intellectual police-force with an authority and powers of guidance that in reality were far less heeded than may appear. The concept of 'return' is the opposite of 'departure'; the departure from order was supposedly brought about by the avant-garde around the end of the nineteenth century and in the early years of the twentieth. But the departure was not simply in one direction; just as order (taken to mean the eclectic system, namely historicism) was not a coherent, unitary order, but complex and contradictory, so there was not just one but a whole system of ways out, or rather a non-system of chinks, avenues, genuine outlets and false exits.

The concept of 'order' is borrowed from architecture itself, where the orders signify a coherent, recognisable morphological system, not necessarily fixed and constant, but rather subject to continually varied interpretations. Metaphorically, 'order' implies Classicism and tradition, bringing into play both historical standards and metahistorical concepts. On the one hand there is the significant weight of the relationship between nationhood and tradition, whether in terms of high culture or vernacular – a national identity to be reappraised against the internationalism of the avant-garde, and ancestral roots contrasted with the comings and goings of stateless persons and those of mixed race; on the other hand metahistorical concepts: order implies geometry, formal structures, 'plastic qualities' (the title of an

Paul Tournon (1881–1965): Drawing of the
interior of Casablanca Cathedral, 1930.

Italian periodical famous in the art world was *Valori Plastici*); qualities specific to the profession, to artistic activity, to the mastery of expressive media, and to art itself.

It is misleading, however, to accuse those active in the 1930s of a return to the past or of readopting eclecticism (even though eclectic veins are never entirely mined out) because the leading lights of the 1930s, from architects to fashion designers (Coco Chanel for one), were convinced that they were working towards something new and modern. For them, the return to order did not mean denying all things modern, but seeking a modernity with its roots (and with them its chances of survival) going deeper than fashion, ephemeral plans, and avant-garde enthusiasms, into the reality and tradition of each European populace in its specific cultural language. Nationalism, the idea of nationhood, had been central to nineteenth-century European history, and the consequence had been historicism, eclecticism. The establishment and political realisation of the new nation states had on the one hand posed problems of national styles representing the idea of nationhood, while on the other within each nation exalting individual qualities, the pluralism of various cultural dialects, regionalism, and local culture.

The twentieth century has been the century of internationalism; the typical member of the avant-garde was a product of the city, his prototype had no roots, pilgrimage was his natural condition, exile his natural sentence; a kind of parallel could be observed between the international socialist movement and the avant-garde.

In the 1930s, nationalism for the first time took solid form as nationalist art. Men like Tristan Tzara were dubbed stateless half-breeds, and internationalism was considered a kind of uprooting. This attitude led to Hitler's racial persecutions, imitated by Mussolini. The decade of the 1930s was pre-eminently the time when the virtues of hearth and home were extolled, *Heimat* and *Heim* were on many German lips, the style of each homeland, each people, was glorified. France, Germany and England witnessed a return to historic styles, the neo-vernacular and the regional, which at the same time aspired to a universal order perceived in the light of Classicism. But is Classicism behind us or ahead? Valéry wrote *Eupalinos*, Cocteau produced *Orphée et Euridice*, Stravinsky composed *Oedipus Rex*. Classicism is not internationalism, nor common models, but the legendary source of every nation, the childhood of humanity, the presence of ancestral origins. Vernacular and universality – this is not an insuperable contradiction, like the antithesis between the German concepts of *Kultur* and *Zivilisation*. National (or worse, nationalist) ideals can only be achieved by means of order. Order implies making distinctions; when creating order the first task is to distinguish and classify; order involves separation. By contrast, the avant-garde movements had sought connection, osmosis, liaison between the major and minor arts, pictorial and decorative arts, architecture and interior decoration, fine arts and fashion, décor and theatre, ballet, and costume design. Since the period of Art Nouveau, the ideal of total art had been pursued, *l'art dans tout*; the artist had rejected the separation and confining of categories, the classification of products and even of techniques. The return to order marked the return to separation. In architecture it involved rationality, the invention of a pseudo-scientific subject, 'the distributive characters of buildings', which laid emphasis on classification and 'typology': architecture could be broken down into public, private, industrial or military. Interior decoration, too, could be categorised: for offices, factories, embassies, ocean liners or private houses. Even the architectonic and figurative languages are recognisable immediately: the rhetorical use that 1930s architecture made of frescoes, mosaics, decorative panels and sculptures emphasises the differences.

The validity of the classifications denied by Croce's aesthetics emerged in a form of 'hierarchy' – a concept beloved of the Fascists – of qualities; the avant-garde were united on the plane of internationalism; they were united too in their desire to break the bounds of the different fields of art. The return to order brought a definition of terms, of national tradition interpreted with nationalistic pride, together with a return to the institutional separation of artistic operations. Order presupposes system, and the return to order represented, on the plane of Alain's pure aesthetics, *Le système des beaux-arts*, published in Paris in 1926 (although written in about 1920), an attempt 'at a strictly designed doctrine of the imagination' which 'should lead not only to the organisation of the fine arts according to human nature, but also to understanding them better and reconstructing them more accurately and, I dare say, physiologically'.

(*top left*) Albert Laprade and Léon Jaussely: ceiling in the Musée des Colonies, Paris, 1931.
(*bottom left*) Auguste Perret: design for the transformation of the Trocadéro, Paris, 1937.

(*inset*) K.S. Melnikov: Detail of the design for the 'Narkomtiajprom' building, Moscow, 1934.

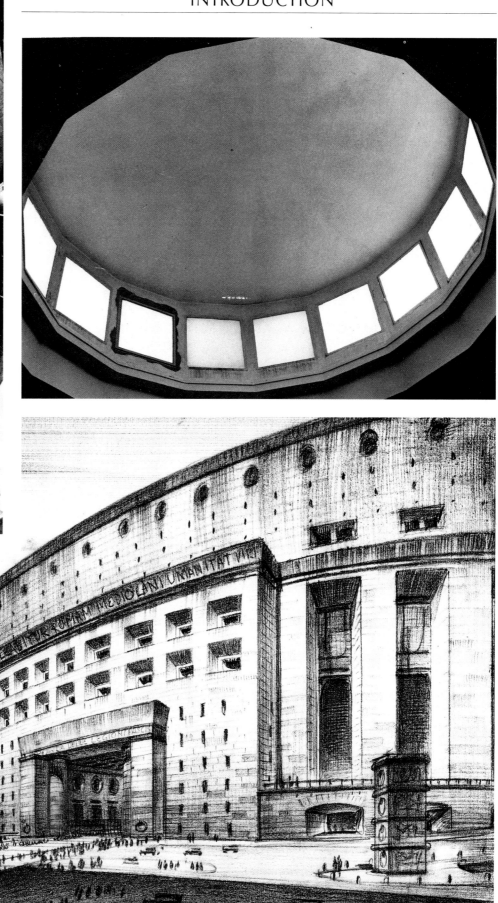

(*top right*) Albert Laprade and Léon Jaussely:
ceiling in the Musée des Colonies, Paris, 1931.
(*bottom right*) Giuseppe de Finetti: design for
the reconstruction of the Porta delle Milizie in
the centre of Milan, 1934.

'EUPALINOS OU L'ARCHITECTE'

Architecture has a vital role to play in the return to order. During the Renaissance it was Alberti, in his *De Re Aedificatoria*, who restored the importance of architecture, proposing a rise in its quality, elevating it from the level of a mechanical art to one of pure intellect, and suggesting that design was the art of mental drawing. A similar reinstatement was achieved during the 1930s, not by an architect or an aesthetic philosopher, strictly speaking, but by the poet Paul Valéry, in his dialogue *Eupalinos ou l'Architecte*. The text appeared in 1921, in a sumptuous volume entitled *Architecture*, printed in a limited edition of 500 copies at the instigation of a group of architects, who invited Valéry to write a preface. The publication can be described as a product of refined arbitrary taste; its graphics were minutely planned, to the extent that the author was asked for a precise number of characters – exactly 115,800. Later, in 1934, Valéry justified his choice of dialogue form, which had seemed to him highly compatible with its contents: 'This precision, surprising and forbidding at first, but exacted from a man fairly accustomed to that of poems with a fixed form, initially made me hesitate, but I then realised that the unusual condition suggested could easily be fulfilled by employing the highly elastic form of the *Dialogue* (with a little experiment, the insertion or removal of a trivial remark enables the fixed metrical conditions to be met).'[1] His account rather tends to explode the reputation of a text that had become gospel; he admits that even the name of *Eupalinos* was a casual choice: 'I found the name of Eupalinos myself, by looking for an architect's name in the Berthelot Encyclopedia under the entry "Architecture". I later learned from the work of the Hellenist scholar Bidez (de Gand) that Eupalinos was more of an engineer than an architect, digging canals and building hardly any temples; I lent him my own ideas, as I did to Socrates and Phaedrus. Moreover, I have never been to Greece and, as for Greek, I have unfortunately always been a very mediocre scholar, who gets lost in Plato's original and finds him terribly longwinded and often boring in translation . . .'[1]

The pointedness with which the author insists on denigrating the cultural and philological elements of the text emphasises its primarily poetic character, his main purpose being to promote architecture to the level of philosophy. Philosophy is basically a question of form; Wittgenstein had asserted that 'every statement is an image', and image cannot be separated from form. Architecture has an advantage over philosophy in that it is able to give concrete expression to thought; architecture can therefore serve as a reference to the

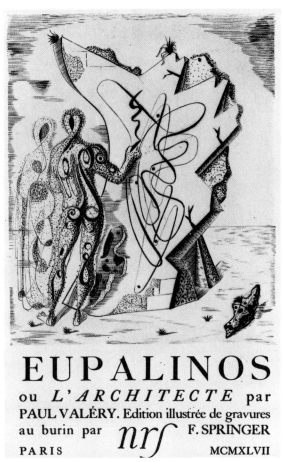

(right) Title-page of a revised edition of Paul Valéry's *Eupalinos ou l'Architecte*, Paris, 1947. The original edition appeared inside the periodical *Architectures*, Paris, 1921 (left).

philosopher because it is a way of realising definite, conclusive forms, and anything added to or taken away from them results in their disturbance or destruction. But such forms are the product of building, so architecture exists above all on the building site. 'You cannot imagine, oh Socrates, what joy such harmonious order afforded my soul; since then I have not been able to distinguish the idea of a temple from that of its building, and when I see one I see an admirable action even more glorious than a victory and more at variance with the poverty of nature.'[2] Seeing architecture means perceiving not an image but a process, an 'action more glorious than a victory'. In the same breath a parallel is drawn here between architecture and the military art, which was summarised in the experience of the Renaissance architects, and which recognises the solitude of the architect as comparable to that of the battle commander. Architecture and military action both occur as a result of the execution by others of decisions made by one responsible person, based on his own knowledge and his evaluation of the situation at a particular moment. Architecture as the art of command, and military command as architecture is an extremely penetrating assessment. 'If destroying and building are of equal importance, and souls are needed for each, yet most dear to my spirit is building.'

This *Eupalinos'* hypothesis embodies all the self-confidence of 1930s architecture as a creative force capable of resolving the evils of cities and educating the public, and, in acknowledging the importance of the building site, it answers the question as to how refined the execution of a design should be. In Eupalinos' maxim: 'Listen. He very often said that in execution nothing may be neglected' – a literary intuition that is also the fruit of extensive experience of building sites. This emphasis on detail leads to preciousness, an élitist element, a formula which embodies the ideals and the taste of the 1930s, in both architecture and the decorative arts.

'"My temple," said the man from Megara, "needs to move men as they are moved by the object of their love."' Architecture's psychological power is a further element that suggests *Eupalinos* as a point of reference for the 1930s. One of the consequences is the rhetorical intensification of the message: 1930s architecture is official architecture, State architecture, whether it is for the Royal Air Force, a Soviet building, or the seat of the French bureaucracy. Even a building such as that in London for the Royal Institute of British Architects itself becomes a symbolic example of the great English professional tradition, at once an exclusive club and a monument to professional pride. This spirit and these values not only invest the monument but monumentalise the detail. There are people prepared to spend months designing a hidden hinge for a cupboard door, juggling veneer round improbable curves, debating the precise choice of new materials to use in interior decoration. Gio Ponti, following the theme of love in *Amate l'Architettura*, defined design as 'practicable thinking'.[3]

Returning to Valéry, we find a distinction between architecture that 'sings', buildings that are 'dumb', and those that 'merely speak'. This is the same as that tradition of 'speaking architecture'[4] of the visionary architects of the Enlightenment, involving a relationship between sign and meaning, purpose and style, architectonic model and formal language; psychological power is no longer merely an individual feeling, but a collective message, 'public' as against 'private', sometimes even intimidation in the name of justice and of institutions. But architecture 'sings' only when it achieves the quality of poetry and music. And behind all this, reminding us inexorably of Le Corbusier's contemporaneous architectural experiments, is the reference to the cultivation of proportion, the parallel between music and architecture, and the common roots of harmony and mathematics.

All these elements – the psychological power of architecture, the poetic quality of the building site, and the all-important detailing – are aspects of the reinstatement, the insistent intellectual promotion of architecture following a long period during which architecture had been reduced to extravagance, ornament and fashion. The whole dialogue is based on the spiritual quality of building, on the process of building as a process of cognition, transforming natural shapelessness into deliberate form, into architecture. The responsibility of form, in the case of architecture, is an all-round responsibility, creating the possibility not of one single point of view, but a realisation conditioned by movement. Consider the processional value of certain churches, or the organising, aggressive quality of some public buildings, such as those of the 1930s in Hitler's Germany. In short, the quality of container and content is affected by sight lines and movement. This dynamic vision of architecture was reflected in the 1930s in both

Grey Wornum: design
for the RIBA building,
Portland Place, London,
1934 (Artist's impression
by J.D.M. Harvey).

photography and cinema, and their method of interpreting architecture was a way of extolling certain qualities, which in turn would influence the choice of those qualities at the architectural design stage.

'Now, of all acts the most complete is that of building. A work requires love, meditation, obedience to your finest thought, the invention of laws by your soul, and many other things you do not know you possess, but which the work miraculously draws out of you. The work derives from your innermost being, but is distinct from you. If it were endowed with thought it would sense your existence without ever managing to prove it or conceive it clearly. You would be like a God for it. . . . So let us consider this great act of building. Observe, Phaedrus, that the Demiurge, when he set about creating the world, attacked the Confusion of Chaos.

'The process of building can be compared to the phenomenon of the creation of the Universe.

'Before him all was shapeless; in that abyss there was not a handful of material he could gather but was infinitely impure and composed of an infinity of substances.

'He skilfully took up the fearsome mixture of dry and damp, hard and soft, light and darkness that constituted chaos, whose disorder penetrated down to the meanest particle. He sifted the faintly shining mud wherein nothing was pure and all the energies were adulterated to the point where past and future, the accidental and the essential, the durable and the ephemeral, intimacy and remoteness, movement and rest, lightness and gravity found themselves mingled as wine with water when they make a cup. Our sages seek always to approach this state in spirit. . . . But the great Creator did otherwise. He was the enemy of similitudes and the hidden identities that we delight in surprising; he organised inequality.'

In this passage we see the dialectic pairs of 'contrasts' as they would have been written in sixteenth-century language: light – dark, accidental – essential, near – far, durable – ephemeral, light – heavy. Creation is knowledge, and knowing implies distinguishing; defining the opposites implies a recognition of their identity. 'But the builder I now show you finds before him, in place of chaos and primary matter, precisely the worldly order that the Demiurge drew from disorder in the beginning. Nature is formed; the elements are separated; but something enjoins him to consider this work unfinished, and in need of being recast and reinterpreted in movement, in order to satisfy mankind more particularly. He chooses to begin his deed at the very point where God had stopped.'

This is a conclusive view of the building process as the second step in creation, or creation of the second degree. It is suggested that the same process that determined the distribution of opposites to obtain the complex phenomena of natural materials be applied in turn to these very materials – wood, rock, or marble, together with gardens, water, air, and light – using them as the raw materials for that responsible process of creation, the construction of architecture. '"Here I am," says the Builder, "I am the deed. You are the matter, you are the force, you are the desire; but you are separate. An unknown industry has isolated you and prepared you according to its means . . . Now the reciprocal is to come."'

This is the end of Valéry's text. It concludes with an affirmative crescendo; first the building operation moves from the informal to the formal through an awareness of the form that is analogous to knowledge, the process of *gnosis* itself. Then this building process addresses itself to the recondite nature of the harmonies which exist in the products of nature, in a clear disposition, which has its basis in the mathematical and organic laws of nature.

Eupalinos enjoyed a singular success for which it became imitated; Jean Badovici wrote a dialogue to present the realisations of Süe and Marie, and Jean Bayet invented a nocturnal dialogue on the Acropolis to reply to Valéry, reproving him for excessive intellecualisation of the arts; Vaillat and Süe in *Rythme de l'architecture* preached a return to geometric formalism and the mathematical ordering of space; Le Corbusier in *Vers une architecture* proposed a modular system and a return to the schemes of the father of French architecture, Choisy. In addition, the text of *Eupalinos* generally proved a splendid tonic for the rôle of the architect in the 1930s. Although, however, the architect confidently presented himself as the one person capable of producing beneficial results for mankind by his planning activity, the myth of the demiurgic architect was subsequently strangled by the politicians, as a result of their irresponsible and unscrupulous use of technicians, and by their incomprehension of or vagueness about architectonic culture. It was this generation though that founded university faculties of architecture, putting the teaching of architecture on a level with that of the most long-established disciplines. The faith that Le Corbusier proposed in *Vers une architecture* as an alternative to the Socialist revolution – *'Architecture ou révolution? Architecture!'* – the belief that human conditions could be improved, that the evils of the world could to some extent be redeemed by the work of the architect, found its ratification, albeit by way of a poetic digression, in the evocation of the very foundation of Classicism contained in *Eupalinos*, namely of harmony as substantial agreement between the laws of nature and those of artistic creation. No longer the 'accursed avant-garde',[5] the protest and the disorder, but work in substantial accord with the natural harmony of things.

More than half a century separates us from Valéry's text, from its imitations, and from that surge of faith largely betrayed by the reality it triggered off, but it remains an extraordinary testimony to the rapport between architectural aesthetics and the thought of the period, an integration of architecture and culture which has never quite been repeated; in fact the thread has been lost. Today it is not so important to ponder on the demiurgic rôle of architecture, because it can no longer be seen to have such a rôle, nor on the rôle of one possible version of Classicism among the many types of Classicism to which we continually have recourse. But it is still important to consider carefully the nature of the building activity, the quality of the architect's responsibility for form, the process of design as a means of and potential for knowledge: knowledge of reality, an uninhibited knowledge free from all obedience to ideologies which are by now in crisis, and from the dogmatics of a Modern Movement that is also largely in crisis.

ARCHITECTURE
AND
REVOLUTION

In *Vers une architecture* Le Corbusier asks the rhetorical question *'Architecture ou révolution?'*, suggesting a positive or negative response to the demands of industrial society, but the faith expressed in his final phrase, 'The revolution can be avoided', remains largely betrayed, the attempt having repeatedly been abandoned by the old European democracies. During the 1930s another dual concept was coined, architecture *and* revolution. The Communist revolution in Russia, the Fascist revolution in Italy, and the Nazi revolution in Germany all needed architecture to bequeath a new image to history, and to offer contemporary society a strong rallying point. For their part the architects and architectonic culture needed revolution to consolidate their programmes, to commit them to an aim, to provide a link between 'personalities' and groups. Naturally there are considerable differences between the Fascist and Communist revolutions, and between the mentalities of the dictators. There are likewise differences in their historical development, and the relationship between modern architecture and revolution. Both the Fascist and the Communist systems embodied the myth of the avant-garde, Futurist in the one case, Constructivist in the other. They flourished on the dynamism of the revolutions, and then abandoned them with a change of course. In Italy this involved nefarious dealings, amid manoeuvres to win favours and decisions from Mussolini, and was associated with the rise and fall – the 'changing of the guard' as the saying went – of the various hierarchies who also commissioned architecture. In Soviet Russia the change was more drastic but carried out within a political debate, through a most complex relationship with the intellectuals, during a succession of Communist Party congresses.

In both cases the result was the same: the abandonment of the modern style in favour of a Classical, monumental style, naively and roughly inspired by *romanitas* in Fascist Italy, and more directly linked to the historical language of bourgeois and proletarian art in Communist Russia. In 1922, Karel Teige wrote: 'If proletarian art is to conserve its positive rapport with its own class (which was not necessary for bourgeois art, which terrified the bourgeois) it will have to ask itself what will be expected of it by the proletariat, which has up to now been a precultural social stratum. It would be difficult to guess what postulates socialist society will pose to art in a consolidated post-revolutionary situation.'[1]

For a few years Italian rationalist architects naively believed they were interpreting the Fascist look by keeping up a controversy against the 'academic' front, which they regarded as the losers. The academicism in question was the legacy of nineteenth-century bourgeois eclecticism and cautious aesthetic ventures accomplished under the aegis of Giolitti[2] – a politician who was never remotely aesthetic; the examples of his 'Italietta',[2] were contrasted with the virile, rational, modernist, 'revolutionary' dynamism of Fascist Italy. The cost of this ingenuousness was to be the break up of the various architectural groups and the loss of the dynamism which stemmed from Futurism; they finished up on opposite sides, sometimes even changing sides, resulting, for example, in the tardy anti-Fascist opposition of figures like Giuseppe Pagano.[3]

In Russia the avant-garde was worn out, or rather wiped out, by the distinction drawn between true proletarian art and popular art, above all between architecture and 'artistic industry . . . conducive to the formation of a sociology of art' (Teige). There was a far-reaching attempt to interpret the concept of Constructivism as involving construction in a non-aesthetic way; the new art would cease to be art, but become a programme for living, immersed in everyday life far from the 'shrines of art', involving proletarian participation instead of being delegated to the intellectual minority or to professional designers. The outcome of all this was that Russian architecture emerged as Stalinesque monumentality.

The last dictator to achieve power, Hitler did not have the problem of the contradictions endemic in Italy and Soviet Russia. He immediately addressed himself to the questions of the precise function of art and the monolithic vision of architecture, ideas not entirely divorced from certain ingredients of modern German aesthetics from Expressionism onwards.

'In my judgement the greatest of all arts is architecture because it comprises them all,' declared Mussolini in his conversations with Ludwig.[4] His alleged *romanitas* emerged at the end of the decade, on the eve of war, in his great dream of the marble city and the colossal E'42, the world exhibition planned to celebrate twenty years of Fascism, at once ephemeral and permanent; but 1942 was the year that led instead to El Alamein, the immediate prelude to his military and political downfall.

FASCIST ITALY

Italian historians have been hard put to it to distinguish good from bad in arguments about the Modern Movement, the works and the designers worth saving and those not, whether Modernism should lose out to eclecticism; it has been a struggle to evaluate Pagano against Piacentini, Libera and Terragni against Vaccaro, but, with an effort, a kind of *a posteriori* verdict of 'not guilty' has been reached: among the works of the Fascist régime not all were broken-winded rhetoric; many, like its industrial products, were the expression of a modern Italy, an Italy that, despite sympathy with and toleration of Fascism, was still a country capable of keeping in step with the times; and the quality of Italian architecture, despite the régime under which it was built, was not inferior to that in the rest of Europe. By a series of circumstances that from time to time upset 'the party game', this was the period when Florence station was constructed – with the approval of Mussolini and the intervention of his girlfriend, the journalist and art critic Margherita Sarfatti, authoress of the book *Dux* and high priestess of the Italian Novecento in painting – and when towns like Sabaudia were built in the Pontine Marshes; both were models of town planning and architectural language.

Eventually, after years of ideological condemnations, of naive distinction between narrowly partisan 'squadristic', Farinacci[5]-style Fascism and imperialist broken-winded, E'42-style, or of flirting with the intimate, introspective, exclusive, elusive values of Novecento art, Bottai[6]-style, there came a phase in which ideological values were put on one side in order to re-evaluate aesthetic and technical elements. One tends to forget that ideas are not to be viewed entirely in terms of black and white. It is not really a question of certain buildings deserving to be preserved while others are totally rejected. In the 1930s there was a mixture of opportunism and faith, compromise and rigour, which shaped an Italian version of monumentalism stimulated by and consistent with Fascism, and, because of the simple fact that in that period Fascism was at its most popular, it was able to entertain the co-existence side by side of avant-garde and tradition, of the monumental and the vernacular.

The concepts tossed around were in fact pseudo-concepts, such as 'Mediterranean character' or 'metaphysical purism', or spontaneous and rural architecture. In short, Italy found a way of being part of the Europe of the 1930s which reflected both the shortcomings and the qualities of Italian culture; it was able to appease the propagandist side with the escapist formalism of magazines, with titles like *Stile, Arte Mediterranea, Aria d'Italia* and *Civiltà* – the last (meaning 'Civilisation') being devoted to E'42.

The Italian kaleidoscope, although so modest when its origins are examined, was nevertheless composed of the selfsame concerns as those current elsewhere in Europe: the same insistence on monumentalism, institutional expression, formal purism, nobility of material. These all had the effect of imposing conditions on architecture: the renunciation of reinforced concrete, an end to metal construction, the promotion of the use of marble by way of homage to Apuania, which Mussolini promoted to the status of province in order to placate

Gruppo Toscano:
Florence Station, 1933:
(*above*) Artist's
impression of the
design, taken from a
supplement of the
periodical *Eclettica*.
(*below*) View of the
'Royal Pavilion' with the
marble sculpture
representing the valley
of the River Arno.

anti-Fascist and anarchic feelings. Glancing at *Architettura d'Oggi* (Architecture Today), a small book by the Italian academician Marcello Piacentini which came out in 1930 as part of the *Prisma* collection (edited, not surprisingly, by the then omnipresent Margherita Sarfatti), we read how Italy regarded the rest of Europe, through the eyes of a man who was the major protagonist of the régime's architecture, but at the same time was able, intelligent, and heir to an eclecticism always *à la page*. In his conclusion he writes: 'I see our contemporary architecture in a setting of great composure and perfect measure. It will accept the new proportions permitted by new materials, while always subordinating them to that divine harmony which is the essence of all our arts and our spirit. It will agree more and more to renounce empty formulae and colourless repetitions, and embrace absolute simplicity and sincerity of form, but it will not always be able to reject as a matter of principle the caress of a suitable decoration.'

Marcello Piacentini (1891–1960): (*top left*)
Headquarters of the Ente Nazionale per
Mutilati e Invalidi di Guerra. (*top right*) Victory
Monument, Bolzano. (*below*) Entrance to
University City, Rome, 1935.

Whereas the text is critically naive, the choice of illustrations is shrewd – at least where Piacentini's capacity for visual assimilation is most obvious; we find there a way of reading Europe that contains everything and the opposite of everything, and in which the artificially constructed distinction between the Modern Movement and contemporary eclecticism finds no place. On the contrary, he finds a certain link between the Milan of Gio Ponti and Baldassare Lancia, the Trieste of Pulitzer, the Stockholm of Hoffberg, the Paris of Auguste Perret, and the Germany of Emil Fahrenkamp and Dominikus Böhm, while taking a 'Constructivist-Novecentist' view of Russia, of the Germany of Hans Poelzig, Walter Gropius and Wilhem Kreis, the Holland of Johannes Duiker and the France of Victor Bourgeois and the latest Henri Sauvage. The possibility of a co-existence between neo-eclectic historicism (in purist-classicist terms) and modernism (in rational constructivist terms), was realised in his work as director of Rome's University City, and is further endorsed by an independent text, Platz's *History of Architecture*,[7] the least translated of the histories of contemporary architecture, not surprisingly, since it disagrees with the rising ideology and also the historical falsification of the Modern Movement. The *Stilbildung* that Platz attributes to architecture found its roots in the constructive spirit of the dialogue between architect and engineer, and in the constructive logic of new materials. It was open to the most modern expressions, but amply assimilated the Expressionist lesson and that of master-builders like Poelzig, Behrens and Fahrenkamp; in short it proposed the three-way partition of architecture into representative, official and monumental; industrial or functional and structuralist; and private (with which Platz does not concern himself further in his text), that is to say traditional, vernacular, *Heimatstil*, which was to form the basis of the Nazi concept of architecture.

NAZI GERMANY

When the Nazis came to power, they did not immediately concern themselves with architecture, but once their social consolidation was complete they used it to celebrate their image. So the period of Nazi architecture is even briefer than the short twelve years of Nazi power. It nevertheless consists of two phases between about 1936 and 1940, first the great set-pieces of party edifices, followed during the war, on a fanatically megalomaniac scale, by plans for Berlin, Nuremberg and Munich, the key cities of the Third Reich. The unusual thing about the rapport between Nazism and architecture is that it existed largely within the minds of two central personalities, Hitler and Albert Speer, involving a close relationship between the dilettante architect-client and the executive interpreter. This was not a situation entirely new to history, but the way in which it materialised was, Hitler becoming a kind of project manager, a rôle he had dreamed of since his favourite architect, Troost, died and he considered taking over his studio. Troost's widow continued to exercise her influence, for example in the treatment of Bonatz; he had made his debut in 1919 with his design for Stuttgart station, a piece of monumental historicism that should have earned him a place among the interpreters of Nazi monumentality, but Troost's widow had him relegated to the technical world of the Todt organisation[8] and to the building of motorway bridges.

Hitler had some practical knowledge and considerable graphic ability, as his sketches confirm, but many episodes in his private life show that his demoniac fanaticism was combined with impulses towards petit-bourgeois conformity, and in art, which was after all his hobby, he gave no sign of anything other than idealised forms, conventional chocolate-box pictorialism, flat technique and academic style. He developed larger-scale ideals of architecture after his visit to Paris, so often reported in film documentaries; he saw it for the first time in a gloomy dawn after the 1940 invasion, and its spaciousness inspired him with the spirit of grandeur and the naive notion of durability; architecture was to carry the image of the thousand year Reich, the elements of which are examined in masterly fashion by Elias Canetti in his essay *Potere e sopravvivenza*.

As for Speer, the young pupil of Tessenow, he showed ever-increasing signs of organising ability and level-headedness, rising from Inspector-General of Buildings to Minister for Armaments, and ensuring Germany's weapons production, including maximum output of tanks and aircraft, during the last years of the war, in spite of heavy bombing by Allied aircraft; there is also historical evidence, confirmed by the Allies, that he safeguarded the elements of Germany's post-war reconstruction by relocating industrial production in out-of-town bunkers. He possessed extraordinary vision and the ability to immerse himself in the joy of planning as the high point of organisation. These same qualities enabled him, during his long detention in Spandau, to interpret the steps he took round the courtyard at recreation time as those of an imaginary journey which he charted on an atlas, enabling him over the years of imprisonment to complete a walking tour of the world in his mind. This is a good example of the mentality that did not

Paul Bonatz (1877–1951): Stadthalle, Hanover, 1911–14.

shrink before any task assigned to him in the tidal wave of enthusiasm generated by the Führer's magnetism.

Apart from this, he was critically and culturally fairly simple, as he showed in conversations I had with him after his release. Not that he despised all modern architecture; on the contrary, he confessed that Behrens' St Petersburg Embassy was a favourite of his and Hitler's too, likewise that he felt a certain trust and admiration for Mies van der Rohe, whose essentiality and reduction of architectonic language under the slogan 'less is more' must have struck him as consistent with his own rhetorical-monumental simplification of masses. He held a number of naive beliefs, such as that the history of architecture was in essence based on the modification of windows, according to the overworked concept of the harmony of masses and spaces. He subscribed to the ideas of Schinkel, whose work he interpreted as indigenous Classicism, the most elevated and the most appropriate to modern-day living. He believed in the superiority of the Ancients, the Greeks above all, not because of his liking for poetry – he was at that time re-reading Hölderlin – but for their practical achievements; he had sent teams of archaeologists to carry out observations on such things as Vitruvian *temperaturae*, those optical corrections of classical monuments, or to take certain measurements – with the object, naturally, of outdoing them. The essential facets, in fact, of Nazi architecture were grandeur and durability, a double challenge to both space and time. It challenged space by making people move within it, by intimidating them, and by creating through the manipulation of public crowds

Paul Ludwig Troost (1878–1934): (*top left*) Kunsthaus, Munich, 1933–7. (*bottom left*) Ehrentempel, Munich, 1933–4.

Albert Speer (1905–81): Colonnade of the Zeppelin-Feld, 1935.

Albert Speer (1905–81): (*top right*) detail of
the Ober-Kommando der Wehrmacht, Berlin,
1940. (*bottom right*) detail of the tambour of
the Grosse Halle, Berlin, 1937–40.

the fideistic idea of kindling, of converting support into fanaticism. It challenged time by entrusting its message to history through the durability of its technology and materials, using granites in the Egyptian style, turning every piece of architecture into a kind of memorial, like funeral monuments in a melodramatic vision of cities that were no more than immense graveyards.

Designing this architecture was simply a matter of delivering the challenge to space and time. The spatial effects were meticulously calculated, while working out a technology for eternity on a basis of historical and archaeological knowledge; even slave labour was revived for building, drawn from the European ranks of forced labourers. Probably at no time in history has architecture been entrusted with tasks more instantly meaningful than the construction of the New Chancellery, intimidating image of that period of threatening negotiations that led to the Munich appeasement, the glorification of the *physis* as the aesthetic moment of the masses, the structures in Nuremberg, and finally the fabulous Triumphal Arch designed in 1941 based on direct suggestions from Hitler. The colossal structure is nothing more than an opportunity to contemplate death, bearing as it does the names of the fallen in all the wars, knowing that Nazi power was consolidated in death, and that only death justified its existence and conferred its sacred aura. Let us read what Elias Canetti says about it: 'Victory shall be celebrated by a triumphal arch, twice the size of the one granted to Napolean for all his victories. This clearly manifests the intention to outdo Napoleon's victories. Since it is expected to last for ever, the arch shall be made in hard stone. But in reality it is made of something more costly – 1,800,000 dead. The names of each one of these fallen shall be sculpted in the granite. In this way they shall be honoured, and also closely united, more closely than would ever be possible in a crowd. In their enormous numbers, it is they who constitute Hitler's triumphal arch. They are not the dead of his latest war, the one he wished and planned, rather those of the first, in which he himself, like every other man, was a soldier. *He* has survived them, but he has remained faithful to them and never disowned them. From the knowledge of those dead he has drawn the strength never to admit the outcome of this war. They were his masses when as yet he had no other, and he senses that it is they who have enabled him to seize power; without the dead of the First World War he would never have existed. His intention of gathering them together in his own triumphal arch is a recognition of this truth and his debt towards them. It remains, however, *his* arch and will bear *his* name. It will be difficult for anyone to read many of the other names; and even if 1,000,000 names really are inscribed, the great majority of them will never be given a thought. What will remain in the memory will be their number, and that enormous number belongs to *his* name.'[9]

Here can be observed the other aspect of the function of architecture in Nazism, namely the rapport between ephemeral and durable, which happened to be the origin of Speer's fortune. As in all dictatorships, and as is inevitable in all mass revolutions, there is the myth of the feastday. The feastday demands the setting aside of the secular in favour of the sacred, physically determines the outlines of

Albert Speer: German pavilion at the Paris International Exhibition of 1937.

the ideology, measures its powers of persuasion and intimidation, and feeds on symbols, substituting them for the dialogue of reason. The Nazi calendar was crammed with rites; the day when power was seized, the anniversary of the founding of the party, Adolf Hitler's birthday, heroes' remembrance day, labour day, and the feasts of the summer and winter solstices were some of the pretexts for instigating mass rites.

Some cities then provided the sites for idealist pilgrimages, because the party's history in terms of religion and mysticism had to be promoted not only in time, with the recurrence of annual rituals, but also in space, moving people towards special places, thus reinforcing the colossal dimension by convergence and attributing to certain places the significance of sacred goals. So from its original beer-halls it emerged into the great forums; but the men remained the same, and in order to complete their symbolic design, already much inspired by the Middle Ages, left-wing symbolism and schematic militarism (not without its own aggressive elegance in uniforms, decorations and banners) they resorted to nocturnal functions, torchlight processions and searchlight gatherings to scrutinise the sky and at the same time show the strength of the Reich's anti-aircraft defences. I asked Speer if this was an evocation of the German spirit's perennial romantic nocturne, a permanent expression of Nazi aesthetics. No, he replied, it was simply that it was impossible to make the pot-bellied Bavarians with their huge belts goose-step in broad daylight without inviting ridicule, whereas the night hid every blemish and made each man a torch. The mass rallies provided an opportunity to measure architecture against a new material, namely human material; in a relationship of mutual violence space was to engulf the masses, giving the individual the measure of his annihilation, and the masses were to dominate and fill the space, denoting, in their capacity as a mass, the measure of their acquired power.

One man alone placed himself in the equation with the masses as one silhouetted against a great number. For the Führer was reserved a space of privilege, the point of convergence, the focus of every composition. He alone presented himself as the fixed object against the moving force of the masses, or, conversely, as dynamism confronting mass immobility. The gestures and the words amplified in space, in that frenetic incantation known as the Führer's speech, are well documented and never cease to amaze for their naive, extravagant folly. All this was architecture too, and architecture in a new-found dimension, for even though the historical precedents, from the celebrations of the French Revolution to all the ephemera of despotism, were precedents of some interest and cogency, bourgeois architecture had forgotten or ignored them.

B. Yofan, V. Schtiouko
and V. Gelfreikh:
Winning design from
the competition for the
Palace of the Soviets,
Moscow (second round),
1931–32.

COMMUNIST RUSSIA

'Moscow, once a melancholy medieval city, Matuska in white stone, reduced to desolation by the war, its buildings affected by Communism, war and hunger, is today turning into a cosmopolitan capital, a lively and noisy centre of culture, manufacture and commerce. This intricate, non-geometrical city, the red Capitol, metropolis of Communism and fortress of the International, is to become the cradle of the new art, the art of the social future.'[10] The personality game is not important, architecture 'must be impersonal because it is not the work of one single person, but the symbol of a community bound by a common ideal'.[11] The architecture programme is too demanding to be left to architects; after all, Hitler himself, taking up a passage of Gottfried Semper, realised that 'when a new idea imposes itself, and as such is accepted by the collective conscience, there it finds architecture at its service, able to translate the ideology into monumental constructions. Architecture's powerful civilising capacity has always been recognised; it is therefore wittingly that the seal has been given to its consecration as a symbol of the dominant social, religious and political system. But it has never been the architects themselves who have supplied the impetus necessary to fulfil this function, but rather the regenerators of society.'[12]

In the main the facts are known; in their internal implications and deep causes they remain mysterious, like much of the Russian soul. In the 1930s the most momentous change of course in the history of public commissioning occurred in architecture. The Soviet Union, the country of successful socialism, had witnessed the alliance (or at least its beginnings) between the avant-garde and revolution. It had initiated the realisation of a language heralded by many fanfares as the one that outstripped all the narrowmindedness of the bourgeois clientèle. These clamours had attracted the European intelligentsia to Russia, ready and eager to serve the new régime, courageously determined, in the name of its own socialist faith and the dogma of aesthetic programmes and manifestos, to confront limitless space, the herculean task of transforming the old peasant Russia into a modern industrialised country. After all this, however, the USSR and the Communist Party renounced the avant-garde and proclaimed a State art which, under the terse and all-embracing formula of 'Socialist Realism' – even more dogmatically and rigidly professed on the wave of the Red Army's victory in the Second World War – brought about a total reversal of policy in favour of an eclectic, historicist, Classicist language, which the modernists considered 'reactionary'. The progressive realisation of the Socialist revolution coincided with the establishment of a reactionary architectural language, and Stalin's dictatorship was expressed in architecture by a gigantic monumentality not much different from that of his ally against Poland, Adolf Hitler.

The philosophical, critical or political justification for this astonishing phenomenon has been the source of rivers of ink attempting to explain or reconcile what appears to be an enormous contradiction: what actually lay at the heart of the new 'modernism', on which discussion was not permitted? But beyond the innumerable written pages, the analogies between specific situations in literature, the fine arts and architecture, beyond the misunderstandings, the compromises, the unavoidable self-criticism, the desperate overtures and the heavy conformism, there remains an immense sum of pain, disappointment, intellectual blood, frustration, enforced reticence, tactful evasion and illuminating conversions produced by the event both in Russia and elsewhere in Europe. It remains one of the most sensitive pages of twentieth-century history, not helped by the difficulty in tracing documents, nor by the great number of ideologies encountered while studying it and attempting to clarify it. In Joseph Roth's *Flight without End*, the alienation of his hero, Franz Stunder, is the consequence of the author's disappointment after his journey to Russia. 'Official Communism fails to recognise the natural unity between the body and its skin, cloth and clothes, and calls it "bourgeois" to believe in this unity, and "revolutionary" to despise form, whereas it has not the slightest feeling for form itself. In consequence, it packages new ideas in the language of the world of bourgeois mediocrity, the very world it wanted to destroy, so becoming more its heir than its grave digger.'[13]

The painful experience of Lukács – his gigantic struggle to remain within orthodoxy in spite of the deviations and heretical urges aroused by his ceaseless reflection on Western thought, which exposed him to continual arguments – is another tip of the iceberg above the impenetrable depths of these events. An even deeper mystery shrouds the suicide of Mayakovsky.

Architecture does not at first sight reflect these lacerating contradictions and sufferings, being based on a pragmatic dynamism with its roots in reality, and even enjoying a certain early exemption from official restrictions and the party's theocratical positions. In contemporary accounts it enjoys the easy criticism that derives from a simplificatory discrimination; on the one hand the forces of renewal summed up in the Constructivist phenomenon and the contribution of European personalities from the architecture of Weimar up· to Le Corbusier, and on the other the reactionary, monumental, new 'academicism', erecting its gigantic edifices to glorify the Stalinist era. It is easy to heap praise and criticism.

The complexity of the debate goes back a long way, and can even be found in the writings of Trotsky in the 1920s, when he argued that it was impossible to maintain the independence of the aesthetic factor, and stated: 'For the materialist, religion, law, morals and art are all single aspects of the substantially unitary process of social development. Politics, religion, law, ethics and aesthetics may be complex facts, differentiated by their social base, and have reinforced and articulated their own specific aspects, but they all remain functions of socially bound man, and are subject to the rules of his social organisation.'[14]

But Trotsky (whose books were prudently removed from Lukács' shelves by his friends and thrown in the river) had seen lucidly that the dynamism of his own period was concentrated in politics. 'Revolution saves society and culture,' he wrote, 'but uses the most cruel surgical procedures. All the active forces are concentrated on politics and on the revolutionary struggle, but all the rest drops into second place, and anything that stands in the way is pitilessly trampled underfoot.'[15] But he also announced that beyond the base struggle for profit there is a stimulating, dramatic and passionate struggle, which mobilises public emotion and individual competition about the new problems: 'All spheres of life – working the soil, planning human dwellings, creating theatre, developing methods of social education for children, solving scientific problems, creating a new style – will enthuse each and every one of us.'[16]

It is hard to know to what extent all this may have been realised or not in the weighty pronouncements of the bureaucracy. Reality and utopia are at odds in the process of the formation of proletarian art and architecture, in the faith in a rationalisation process which may tackle immense problems with limited means, in the conviction that architecture is a determining element in social reconstruction. The facts are well known: on the one hand, the extension of architecture into town planning with rational faith in the planning activity and in the

(*above*) I.A. Fomin: Moscow Underground, Krasny Vorota Station, 1935. (*below*) Vesnin brothers: design for the competition for the People's Commissariat for Heavy Industry, Moscow, 1934.

real power that socialist society assures this instrument; on the other, the symbolic needs, as depicted in certain key episodes, Tatlin's spiral (which was rejected), the competitions for the Kharkov theatre and the Palace of the Soviets, the Moscow underground railway, the great monumental structures of Stalin's Moscow. In 1932 CIAM (Congrès international d'architecture moderne) refused to hold their congress in Moscow and deliberately chose to weigh anchor in Marseilles and head for Greece and Athens, the land of Classicism; from that year onwards modern architecture was divorced from Russia for the next quarter of a century. Soviet architects became locked in verbal discord and controversy between quite prominent associations such as SNOVA, VOPRA, OSA and MAO, reproducing the disagreements of writers and artists about rejection of the West, the origins of the proletariat, and accusations of formalism. Party and government remained aloof, limiting themselves to calling in some West Europeans: Hannes Meyer and Ernst May (namely the Bauhaus and the Frankfurt Group with their rational use of prefabrication), Van Loghem and Mart Stam from Holland, Jaromir Krejcàr from Czechoslovakia and André Lurçat from Paris. By concentrating on technology, it was possible to by-pass the continual arguments about form and content, artistic autonomy and the dictatorship of the proletariat.

It is Lurçat who gives the most precise report on the Soviet situation. He was not given a technical task or required to work out a rational planning model, but was asked to define the rôle of architecture in the USSR. In an important article entitled *Retour d'Union soviétique*, published in *Art vivant* in 1934, Lurçat writes: 'So we arrive at the second stage of architectural development in the USSR. It is a particularly interesting period, because now it is no longer simply a case of utilitarian buildings, but we are entering the era of great constructions. Numerous monuments are to be erected, entire towns realised, and this time the matter of appearance will assume quite a new importance. Architects are faced with serious questions: these theatres, clubs, Soviet palaces, all these architectural complexes they are asked to carry out, could they be realised in the Constructivist style, this rather primitive style, somewhat too dominated by basic considerations of function?'[17] He clearly reports the gap between the technology available in Russia and the results of Constructivism borrowed from more advanced countries, and with no less clarity condemns the Neoclassic formalism, which 'hides its present impotence beneath columns and capitals, cornices and sculptures,' and he concludes, 'The failure of the former (Constructivists) has not given victory to the latter (Neoclassicists) since, as we have seen, the question is not solely a case of aesthetics, but underneath all this debate we constantly come up against the all-important problem of technological development.'[18]

In a report sent to Kaganovich, president of the Moscow Soviet, Lurçat concludes: 'The Soviet proletariat cannot know all at once precisely what they may desire in the cultural field, so it is difficult for them to indicate that they want this, that or the other artistic form, and research should be done in this direction in order to satisfy them. When it comes to architecture, having no tradition before their eyes

André Lurçat (1894–1970): designs for the competition for the Academy of Sciences, Moscow, 1934. (*above*) View of the Praesidium. (*below*) View of the Library.

but the edifices that express the ideology of the rich bourgeoisie and their already decayed religion, it is easy to understand how the proletariat let itself be momentarily seduced by the false luxury there displayed, without immediately being able to fasten on the errors that it all entailed.'[19]

In the design he submitted in the competition for the Russian Academy of Sciences, also in 1934, Lurçat suggested a compromise between Classical and modern architectural languages based on strict symmetry and cunning perspective; he combined Le Nôtre with Novecento and proposed French grandeur as most befitting the dignity of that great Soviet cultural institution. The idea of the Classical inevitably involved the concept of monumentality. 'If we find constructions built for the public in Ancient Rome,' he wrote, 'analysis at once shows us that the political and social form of Roman society demanded for its own preservation constructions intended for the people for the purpose of distracting them and diverting them away from problems of State.'[20] Here there is no shadow of the Roman public's ancient protest against Pope Sixtus V: 'We want bread, not spires and fountains.' The architecture of successful socialism revives all the despotic and escapist qualities of the *ancien régime*; the monument is the 'expression of the entire social system and therefore available for all to use, in fact the actual symbol of that availability. The architect must therefore turn to the monument to rediscover in it architecture's universal laws, finally all-embracing and totalising. With the assumption of the monument as a design project – the monument which is by definition a non-design, an image, a symbol – we end this survey of Soviet architecture. In the monument, in fact, architecture encounters nothing but architecture; it expresses and defines itself through itself, in a process of self-reflection which is in itself a guarantee of *presence*.'[21]

Lurçat's attempt, no less than Le Corbusier's, remains an isolated episode in the debate within the Russian world; there the architects of the VOPRA, the Union of Proletarian Architects, had branded three enemies – formalism, eclecticism, and Constructivism – and fondly contemplated a proletarian architecture that would be the expression of a new life-style and the means of liberating and educating the masses. But in the event they destroyed themselves with their continual polemics, identifying the political language of party bickering with that of aesthetic criticism, and employing phrases such as 'the kulak roots of the eclectic' and 'those petit-bourgeois of Cubo-futurism', even extending to accusations of Trotskyism and the like. For their part the traditionalists held aloof from any kind of argument and courted fewer risks, until in 1931 the plenum of the Communist Party Central Committee tackled the problem of town planning and improvement. 'Battle is joined to win a new ideological content for Soviet architecture; for the assimilation of all aspects of highly artistic forms, fully satisfying the aesthetic needs of man in socialist society.'[22]

In 1932, the committee for the Palace of the Soviets, presided over by Molotov, announced the results of the competition in a declaration that set out the absolute requirements of monumentalism – simplicity, unity and elegance in architectural expression, together with the need to call 'as much on new creative procedures as on those employed in Classical architecture'.[23] In 1932 the existing literary and artistic associations were 'reorganised' by closing them down.

In 1934 the Academy of Architecture was created; in 1935 Stalin himself inspired and directed the plan for Moscow; in 1937 the first congress of Soviet architects was held, adopting 'statutes' no less, wherein it was reaffirmed that 'Socialist realism is the fundamental method of Soviet architects in the field of architecture; Socialist realism signifies the intimate union of ideological expression and honesty of artistic expression, together with the specific design of each edifice for the technical, cultural, or utilitarian purposes peculiar to itself'.[24] Stalin is credited with having said: 'This generation has made the revolution, so give them what they want; then we shall demolish the lot within ten years.' But this certainly did not mean going back to wooden buildings, to the folk formulas of the 'désurbanistes', but implied the recruitment of specialist workers for the construction of the gigantic Corinthian capitals for the Palladian-Ionic order of the 1934 Joltovsky edifice on the Moskovaia, in order specifically to demonstrate the superiority of Renaissance-style historicism over modern architecture.

Architecture gave up being an ideological instrument in order to become representative and concentrate on the monument. Historicist eclecticism, crystallised into the individuation of specific characteristics in the popular traditions of the various Soviet republics that constitute the USSR, offered a safe road corresponding to the Socialist realism of the fine arts and, in the end, as in all eclectic movements, some imaginative openings in a world of grey conformity and worryingly repetitive authoritarianism. In the wake of de-stalinisation Stalin was blamed for everything; a passage in the *Histoire de l'architecture*

Competition for the Palace of the Soviets,
Moscow, 1931–32. Winning design by
B. Yofan, V. Schtiouko and V. Gelfreikh.

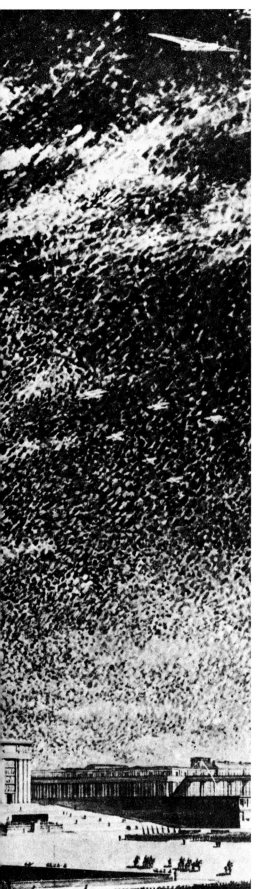

ДВОРЕЦ СОВЕТОВ

(*top to bottom*) Design by A. Joubov,
P. Tchechoulin and D. Smolin. Design by
A. Tchouka. Anonymous design.

43

(*above*) Design by a team of students led by
A. Vlassov. (*below*) Design by S. Guermanovitch.

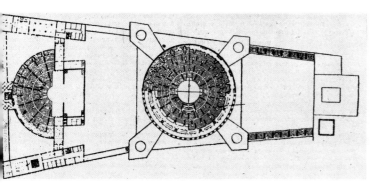

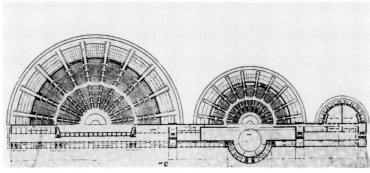

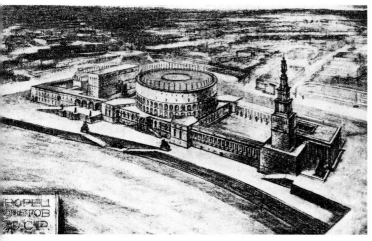

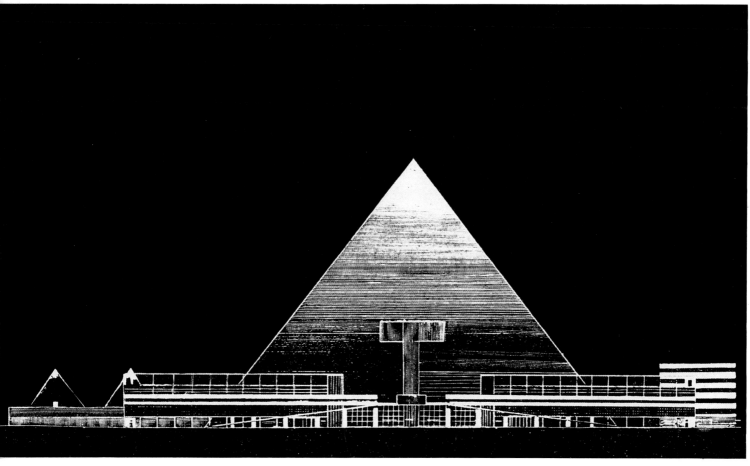

(*top left*) Design by I. Joltovsky (plan and elevation). (*top right*) Design by L. Vichinsky (plan and elevation). (*below*) Anonymous design.

(*top left and bottom*) M. Posokin and
A. Andoiantz: Administrative building in
Moscow, mid-1930s. (*top right*) I. Voltovsky:
Residential block known as 'on the Moskovaia',
Moscow, 1934.

soviétique 1917–1958, published by the Édition d'État pour la construction, l'architecture et les matériaux de construction, Moscow 1962, observes: 'The Stalin personality cult was accompanied by an ever-increasing tendency towards representativity, super-monumentalism and decorative richness, and was partially responsible for pointing architecture in a false and unilateral direction, in defiance of the needs of the Soviet people.'[25]

It is justifiable to include the USSR in the history of Western architecture on the grounds of the continual exchanges, particularly those that led to Diderot's advice to Catherine the Great and to the presence of Western architecture in St Petersburg, making it the crowning city of all the town planning of the Renaissance and the Enlightenment; all the same it must be realised that the involvement remained partial. It is true that the exchanges continued throughout the Revolution and the 1930s, alongside other forms of co-operation, such as the presence of members of the German General Staff as Red Army instructors, but these facts alone do not amount to total involvement in the dialogue taking place in Western Europe.

The problems of industrialisation, the War of the Kulaks – the one Stalin defined, according to Churchill, as graver even than the Nazi invasion, operation 'Barbarossa' – and the great spaces themselves all add up to a situation beyond our normal scope and the usual dialogue between historicist and modernist, Classical style and Novecento as conceived in the 1930s. In the system of popular Russian traditions, in the Russian soul, in the establishment of true Socialism, there remain areas where we find it difficult to comprehend the mystery of that world which Mayakovsky defined as ill-equipped for happiness.

THE MONUMENTAL ERA

TOWN PLANNING

Milan, Paris and Brussels all exemplify the common European tendency to envisage cities on a grand, monumental scale and rebuild them on plans that embodied vitality and hope. This architectural language attempted to integrate geometry with a reassuring balance of masses, drawing inspiration from the traditional plans of Classicism, Greek 'proportion', the lesson of the Beaux-Arts with their junctions, stars and curves, together with the ample perspectives born in the nineteenth century and the predilection for large shapes extolled by Otto Wagner in the early twentieth century.

We know that Hitler took a personal hand in the projects of his architects Troost and Speer, most of whose works, notably Speer's projects for the reconstruction of Berlin, were never realised, but were used nonetheless for propaganda designed to give the people a feeling of unity.

Certain cities such as Milan achieved a coherence and poetic atmosphere worthy of Giorgio de Chirico's *Piazze d'Italia*, imbued with a certain metaphysical aura. In others this was destroyed by vulgarity and over-simplification, and the quest for monumentality led only to empty rhetoric. Many a grand architectural Utopia flourished, with triumphalist town plans in great evidence. The juxtaposition of grandiose edifices with a succession of stepped storeys – as seen here in Sauvage's project for the layout of the Porte Maillot in Paris – evokes the Tower of Babylon. Everywhere there was a manifest desire for grandeur. Architecture merged into town planning but did not become totally identified with it. Only in this sense can we speak of the urban dimension of the monumental order.

Henri Sauvage: Design for the layout of the Porte Maillot, Paris, 1931.

(above) G. Brunfault: Design for the Royal
Albertine Library, Brussels, 1935. (below) Henri
Sauvage: Design for the layout of Porte Maillot,
Paris, 1931.

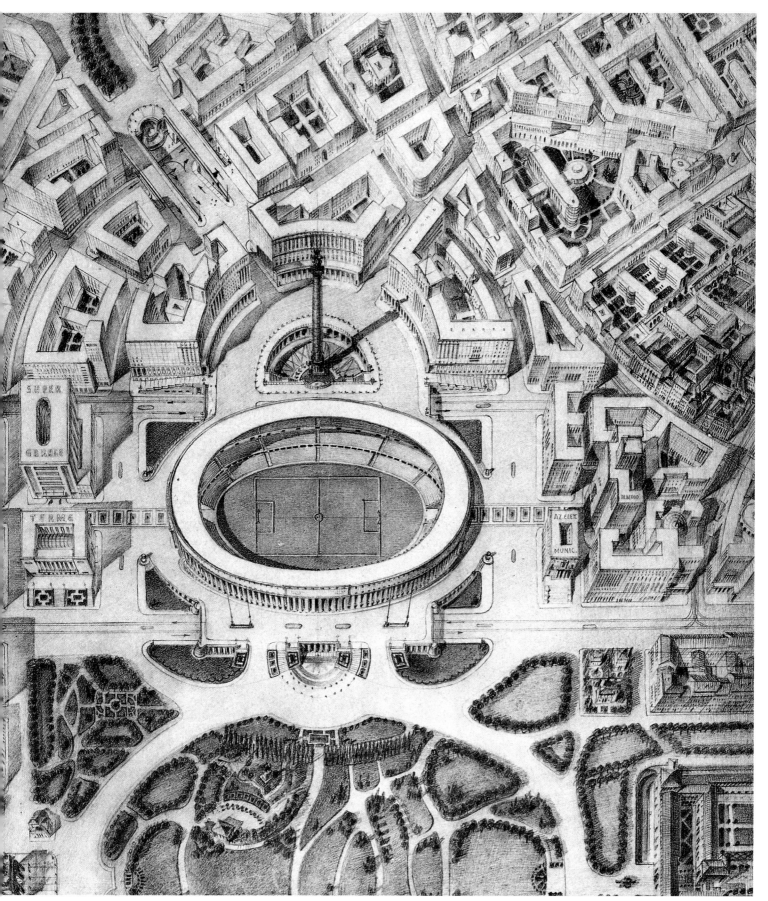

Giuseppe de Finetti: Design for the
restructuring of the Arena district, Milan, 1933.

THE MONUMENTAL ORDER

In the 1930s, parallel with a rethinking in the figurative arts, there emerged in Europe a common architectural language that transcended ideologies and political régimes and in which two factors – realism and tradition – were always present, though in varying degrees.

In architecture the element of order is inseparable from the concept of monumentality. 'Monumental' is an ambiguous word, sometimes simply indicating civic sculptures or funerary masonry, while 'ancient monuments' automatically denotes all historic buildings. But in the sense in which we use it here, the most obvious ingredients of monumentality are spatial amplitude and grand dimensions; there is in addition an implication of refined architecture with a particular message, an impressive psychological effect which can be exerted by the architectural language itself, independent of dimension. Consider, for example, Bramante's small but stupendous temple in the cloister beside San Pietro in Montorio in Rome. 'Essentially the monument is a declaration of love and admiration allied to the highest ideals that bind men together,'[1] wrote Lewis Mumford, adding: 'A period that has repressed its values and lost sight of its aims will not produce convincing monuments.'[2]

Because the architectural language of the Novecento went through a purist phase, when form was simplified and all direct historical quotations were eliminated, there was freedom to concentrate on the quintessential factors that constitute monumentality and to seek to determine their effects. Having once removed the system of symbols comprising decoration, ornamental reliefs and quotation of the canonic orders, one is left with the essential elements of mass, volume, structure, and colour of materials, and can then analyse under what conditions and in what forms their psychological powers can be fully realised. Order by itself is insufficient to create monumentality. The most elementary condition of order is symmetry, but a composition of symmetrical masses is not automatically monumental. Order is repetition, rhythm and balance, but none of these factors in itself ensures monumentality. On the other hand monumentality cannot appear without order; it will not occur in a single case where architecture is spontaneous, organic, vernacular, appropriate to the needs of man and the nature of the landscape; in fact it has no place there, where architecture is a matter of satisfying the demands of everyday private life and meeting a series of functional and psychological requirements to which the notion of monumentality is extraneous.

Sir Edwin Lutyens: Preparatory drawings for two cenotaphs in northern France. (*above*) Monument to the Australian soldiers in Villers- Bretonneaux, 1924–38. (*below*) Monument to those who died in the battle of the Somme, Thiepval, 1923–30.

But where the involvement of the public is concerned, where institutions intend to manifest their dignity, or authorities their presence, or social, commercial or industrial organisations their prestige, then monuments become highly important. The Lingotto FIAT factory and the Karl Marx Hof, no less than the Chilehaus or the Turbinenfabrik by Behrens, are monuments of their age in that they promote rhetorically the significance of their purpose, whether it be the value of the working masses, the power of industry, or economic and commercial prestige. So the State in its ceremonial, symbolic, bureaucratic, institutional or public sectors becomes a major commissioner of architecture, and needs to weight its performance with abstract powers, expressing itself in terms of force, dignity, social effectiveness, even concern about hygiene and efficiency – Tony Garnier's abattoirs at Lyons are a prime example of the latter.

Industrial society produces more monumentality than did the despotic or religious past, because it presents itself as a collection of empires; the modern world, whether capitalist or socialist, needs to confer a visible dignity on these empires, to measure their social power and influence in physical terms, to project in their architecture the tangible image of a powerful social force.

The monumental order is at once the lowest common denominator of a multiple and polymorphic product and the pluralistic result of an attempt to try not to reinforce the present with the authority of history, as in eighteenth-century eclecticism, but to propose it as a new phase of history spanning both historicism and the post-modern; the monumental order takes shape as the modern system or as an attempt to systematise the modern. As such it should not be confused with Neoclassicism or a new form of Neoclassicism or persistent eclecticism, even if it sometimes looks similar.

In the 1930s there was a real faith in the power of aesthetics to exorcise the evils of the world, among which those of the city were predominant. There was a profound conviction that a modern world had to be built, but that there were two different roads to it: the orthodox and limiting route of rationalism and functionalism, basically a new form of positivism determining international style, and that of those who thought it possible to reconcile tradition and history with modernity – 'the fire-fighters' international', as they were dubbed by certain historiographers. The Modern Movement had wiped the slate clean of history and regarded its legacy simply as a decaying academic product. But at a certain point all those who had pioneered the new language confronted the problem of continuity with history, and how to extract from history the qualities that rendered it effective, durable, and monumental. The concept of modernity in the narrow sense has prevented historiographers from attributing validity to this attempt; they dismiss it simply as a conservative compromise or limit themselves to delivering absolutist judgements based on the extent to which it corresponds to the dogma of the Modern Movement. It has in any case been judged and dismissed wholesale, without the components and antecedents being analysed in depth, whereas this has been done exhaustively in research on Art Nouveau and Art Deco, where all the innovative aspects have been examined, the derivations, the influences, the connection with developments in the fine arts, and the results as far as taste and the use of decoration are concerned.

Quite apart from any passion for revival and any temptation to re-evaluate at all costs, I believe that such a broad and multifarious phenomenon deserves a critical exercise of this kind; the post-modern situation, and the presence in contemporary architecture of this same institutional quality, not as a return to the past but as a rebuilding of the present, have created the conditions for it. An attempt in this direction is therefore possible, and I shall try first to trace the internal connections, without too much emphasis on contrasting national characteristics – although these are vividly evident when we come to examine those years – and without giving undue attention to the weight, importance and quality of the personalities involved.

CLASSICISM

The concept of Classicism has been one of modern architecture's formidable rallying points since about 1700, giving rise not only to that phenomenon more generally known as Neoclassicism, but also to a series of references to Classicism in the form of a constant but constantly changing system of references and perspectives. The concept of Classicism can be defined as one of harmony, balance, and permanence beyond passing fashion and avant-garde ephemera. It stands, according to *Eupalinos*, for the intellectual promotion of architecture as a process of knowledge, an unrepeatable historic system of balances between social order and artistic production. Classicism is an ideological aspiration rather than a system of signs, and sometimes it is an escape from the propagandist dictates of totalitarian régimes. Classicism means balance, and the factors of balance consist in a series of proportional relationships and a series of geometric figures. Hoffmann's square, which survives from Art Nouveau into the 1930s, is a prime state of balance: the square has no dynamism, the square is as serene as unity. Even the reading of the Greeks that Le Corbusier gives in his book *Vers une architecture* authoritatively attempts to reduce their lesson to a basic network of relationships and the 'play' of volumes in light.

Stereometric sharpness, clarity, and the prevalence of solid masses are indispensable factors, absolutely fundamental to modern Classicism in the 1930s. But there was a more delicate question – that of the morphology of the orders, the relationship of column to architrave, vertical structure to horizontal. The widespread use of reinforced concrete only emphasised the importance of every calculation involving beam and pillar, but how could this structure and this material be promoted to the dignity of architecture and not turned into a static skeleton to be hidden under decoration? The problem dragged on even into the post-war years. Even though cladding conveniently allows the pipework of installations to be hidden, it adds weight to sections that reinforced concrete could have made slim. Furthermore, if this is faking, then placing in evidence what is there for functional purposes is an act of courage and purity. But concrete, with its wooden moulds and irregular dribbles between joists and planks, is not a very pleasing material, and the haphazard quality of these details works against geometrical purity. There were attempts to eliminate the irregularities by means of pointing, or rather by making use of a form of

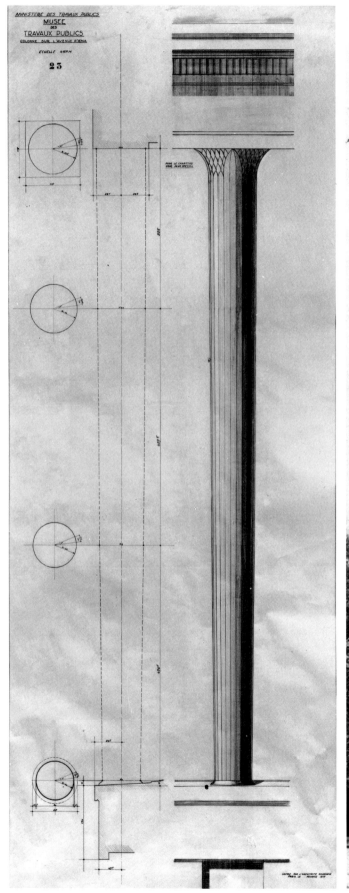

Auguste Perret (1874–1954): Musée des Travaux publics, Paris, 1937. Study for the columns, and view while under construction.

Auguste Perret: Musée des Travaux publics,
Paris, 1937. View while under construction.

Auguste Perret: the 'Mobilier national', Paris,
1931. Inner courtyard and entrance colonnade.

stone-dressing and stopping, but difficulties were encountered with the iron armatures, with parts that were poorly juxtaposed, and with fragile edges and corners, and it was often decided therefore to apply a kind of pebble-dash as exterior cladding. It took a deliberate rough-cast technique to make bare concrete acceptable, apart from a later development which involved in some great works of engineering regaining the sharp lines of Classicism by the use of metal moulds.

It was Auguste Perret who explored the possibilities of fretted concrete, a working technique for making the *pilotis*, the cylindrical pillars, clear and sharp. The reduction of a column to a plain cylinder posed a problem – what to do with the capital and the base? A certain diffidence is discernible here. Eliminate the acanthus leaves, and the capital is reduced to a simple prism looking rather neo-medieval – certainly nothing to do with classical theory. So consideration was given to doing without altogether or to allowing just a small capital reduced to a plain collar, or to eliminating the base, or reducing both to a few details not in any canonic rule, or to eliminating both of them completely. Numerous experiments were made along these lines, from luxurious Parisian buildings in the 1930s right up to Mussolini's E'42. Sometimes, as in Milan in the 1930s, with Muzio, Piacentini, Ponti or Lancia, there was a little less shyness of bases and capitals, and the Classical quotation was maintained, reduced to a simplified Tuscan order, the most austere and basic of the orders. But the problems of the cylindrical column do not end with its extremities; there is also the matter of entasis, which compensates for the optical deformation that makes cylinders appear narrower at the bottom than the top, and which gives rise to an unpleasing funnel-shape. So wherever possible it was essential to reintroduce entasis, and indeed Gropius had used it in his Faguswerk[3] design before 1914.

Classical morphology was not based solely on formal practice, but also on the psychology of form, which is a permanent feature of human perception regardless of period and historical circumstances. The column suggests a connection between width and height, the famous module, and in spite of the thinness and daring permitted in section by the more advanced reinforced concrete, there is a limit to what the eye will accept and find pleasing. At what point does the *pilotis* lose its importance and begin to look like a frail toothpick, even though it is physically in no danger? Exactly when it loses its canonic proportions; it is fatal to deviate very far from them.

Every *pilotis*, even if it starts as a Cubist cylinder, comes back inevitably to being a column. The same may be said of the beam which remains an architrave hower long poured concrete makes it last. Other problems involved are those of section in relation to light, of accept-able balance between ponderousness and frailty, deriving from a section too large or too small, or from the possibility that the mouldings with their parallelism and their light and shade may elevate its continuity above the supports and gracefulness of the section. But how could mouldings be updated? The most obvious way is to reduce their number to essentials, for example by limiting them to those which are employed between frieze and architrave, and by simplifying them, eliminating double mouldings and replacing them with sloping planes, rounding off mouldings, and by carrying out a geometrical

Auguste Perret: Staircase and rotunda of the
Musée des Travaux publics, Paris, 1937.

simplification and reduction of those elements that have an essential chiaroscuro function. The same considerations apply to the pilaster strips and rectangular pilasters, although in this case it is easier. There is a certain compatability between geometric elements based on the parallelepiped and they are able to maintain Classical cadences and rhythms, even in the total absence of decoration and references to the architectural orders. Further possibilities are offered by elongation, allied to the concept of deformation peculiar to modern art, of which more will be said later.

Another problem is the arch. Here there is a basic contradiction. If reinforced concrete structures are always a grid system of beams and pilasters, the arch must always be a fake. If the arch is made out of reinforced concrete, this contradicts the material's plastic continuity. However far back we go, the arch is simply a system for using small elements like bricks or hewn stones; it has geometric continuity but structural discontinuity. With the structural continuity of poured concrete the arch loses its *raison d'être*. But is architecture without arches thinkable? Look at what Garnier did in the Lyons Stadium, where his great arches attain a degree of symbolic sublimity, or at La Padula's 'Square Colosseum', the Palazzo della Civiltà Romana at Rome's EUR, where the constant theme of the arch repeated on all four sides and on all floors creates a certain metaphysical impact. The arch suggests the theme of Mediterranean style as in the cautious and clever new look at sixteenth-century Classicism brought off by Muzio, for example, in the new Catholic University at Milan. The arch also suggests a triumphal quality in colonial architecture, or in the work of someone like Hans Poelzig, a baroque nostalgia. The monumental order, even while preferring the Greek model of Classicism – the system of architraves and lacunae, geometric links based on squares and rectangles – cannot eliminate the *romanitas* of the arch; in buildings of mainly functional character it presents the formal dignity of the parabolic arch, which corresponds most closely to a natural trajectory, the most organic according to the laws of static equilibrium, the furthest from historic geometry; but its use remains conditional on structural functionalism and extraneous to the search for a modern Classicism.

'The real symbolic ornament,' wrote Poelzig for a lecture he gave in 1931, 'the ancient column, is pure music, absolutely non-naturalistic, bearing no relation to nature; even the acanthus on the Corinthian column is not derived from some deliberate stylisation of a natural form, but a new creation on a different plane. It is obvious that such an ornament could not develop in and from the tonal architecture of today; to what extent there will be a fresh attempt to break up the surfaces in a more diverse way from the chromatic and decorative point of view, as opposed to the smoothness that generally predominates today, is really a problem of no importance. It will and must come when saturation with decorative and chromatic monotony increases.'[4]

The old master of constructive objectivity, steeped in industrial architecture, was asking himself a series of questions and posing a series of problems to which it was hard to find an answer. Was 'purism', which in the terms then current only meant 'simplification', sufficiently

Paul Tournon (1881–1964): Interior of the
church of the Saint-Esprit, Paris, 1928.

Hans Poelzig (1896–1936): Designs for the Schauburg, 1932.

(*above*) exterior and (*right*) view of the stage and steps.

effective to ensure the birth of a modern Classicism? Other instances and other worries were pressing. In substance, the new Classicism proposed the prevalence of elementary geometry together with the cerebral and rational nature of architecture (but not only in the functional sense), and refused all forms of romantic mimicry, organicism, or naturalistic inspiration. It indulged rather in mechanicism, in the machine as the product of human rationality and as the achievement of technical progress, and it partly explained its expressive dynamism, above all in design, by proposing a machine aesthetic in the same way as the nineteenth century had proposed an aesthetic based on progress. Urban-based, indifference to site, and intellectual rigour have been common features of Western civilisation. This explains why Europe, in the last phase of its predominance, exported Classicism to the colonies as a sign of superior civilisation, and at the same time imported a taste for the 'primitive', which had stimulated the avant-garde and which was now becoming widely popular.

Dominikus Böhm (1880–1955): (*above*)
Church of St Joseph, Hindenburg (now Zabrze,
Poland), 1938. (*below*) Church of St Elisabeth,
Cologne, 1932.

Wilhelm Kreis: (*above*) Autobahn bridge in Germany, n.d. (*below*) Soldatenhalle, Berlin, 1938–9, with a sculpture by Arno Brecker.

Dominikus Böhm: Church of St Elisabeth, Cologne, 1932.

THE EVOCATION OF GOTHIC

Gothic and Classical are the two key architectural languages of Western civilisation. Their interaction between the Middle Ages and the Renaissance, between the Renaissance and the Baroque, and their revival in eighteenth-century historicism, formed the basis of the history of European architecture. Even during the 1930s the Gothic style was not entirely eradicated, though it survived in a form that involved reinterpretation and which was purged of all suspicion of medieval romanticism and sense of being a quotation. Wherein did this constant Gothic idiom reside? In the separation between skeleton and shell, which was heavily restated by reinforced concrete structures; and in the prevalence of windows, which were incorporated as one of the expressive features of modernism without any functional logic as regards climate. As for architectural language, Gothic implies vertical, and verticality means extension in height – a much sought-after element of monumentality. Gothic also implies rhythm, which leads to reduction of materials, slim structures, audacity – all factors that were systematically reintroduced as part of the vocabulary of the Modern Movement. Gothic was one of the historic factors of nationality – as we see in the dispute over French or German architectural supremacy – and so represented an ancestor of the tradition that had to be recovered, of that German tradition reintroduced by the Third Reich, but which was also present in Expressionism, and was a recurring component of German culture. In more literal terms it meant proclaiming the Gothic tradition in reinforced concrete as the nineteenth century had done in iron.

At the church of St Theresa in Montmagny, Perret explored even in terms of structural decoration the possibilities of a Gothic language compatible with the use of reinforced concrete. Perret has been unfairly left out of contemporary architectural history, or merely celebrated as a pioneer for his house in the rue Franklin and his garage in the rue Ponthieu, but he carried out some particularly interesting work, involving both the Classical tradition and the Gothic, exploring the possibility of re-creating the viability of these two historic languages from within the building process. In his time he carried out a most difficult and thankless task, and did so successfully because he had great flair for building and a sound technique; he seems like a modern Eupalinos proclaiming the building process to be a function of knowledge.

Karl Moser is in a similar situation in the case of the church of St Anthony at Basle, even though his search for spaciousness is more pertinent to modernity, while the coffering of the low vault is reminiscent of Renaissance Classicism. In the churches by Dominikus Böhm Expressionism is dominant in an almost monothematic sense (that is to say there is one key idea in each of them) and the pointed-arch quotations converge with the unity of the surfaces and the parabaloids; in fact, instead of the skeleton being separate from the shell, the roofing is compact; it is corrugated and divided into vaults, reminiscent of Romanesque obscurity and emerging as a kind of theatrical decorativism. An indirect evocation of Gothic is found in German architecture by Issel, Bonatz, Fahrenkamp and Poelzig,

Paul Tournon: Detail of stained-glass window in the church of Elisabethville-sur-Seine, 1928.

consisting mainly of vertical extension, crowded rhythms, and corrugated surfaces. Italy, needless to say, finds the Gothic style alien. Obviously this is not the case in England, where an experimental pluralism was characteristic of architecture in this decade, particularly ecclesiastical architecture, although Gothic in this case does not signify monumental emphasis, but rather the influence of indigenous tradition.

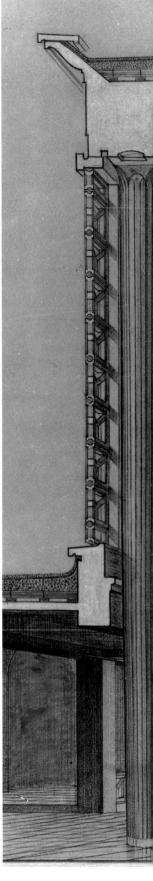

Auguste Perret: Church of St Theresa at
Montmagny, 1925.

Auguste Perret: design for the interior of
St Benedict's Church, Carmaux, 1939.

(*above*) Dominikus Böhm: St Engelbert's
Church in Essen, 1935. View from south-east.
(*below*) Auguste Perret: design for St Benedict's
Church, Carmaux, 1939.

(*above*) Dominikus Böhm: choir of the Church
of the Holy Cross, Dülmen, 1939. (*below*)
Auguste Perret: interior views of the Church of
St Theresa at Montmagny, 1935.

THE CUBIST COMPONENT

The relationship between Cubism and architecture is a delicate question that has remained unresolved critically. On the level of immediate appearance, modern architecture, Novecento style, is to a certain extent Cubist because it celebrates pure volume, the geometry of volumes of which the cube has become the symbol and paradigm, and explores the union between cube and cylinder and sometimes the sphere. But there is a difference between experiments with architectural geometry and real Cubist exploration. It is impossible for architecture to provide simultaneous perceptions. Painting can reject universal perspective, but architecture remains permanently bound to it, because it is inevitably perceived in perspective. In painting, the perception of different perspectives may be simultaneous, but in architecture they can only be successive, and it is movement which conditions its rhythms and its succession of images. In painting, the resolution of the 'analytic' moment is synthetic, while in architecture the perception is analytic and the design a moment of synthesis. This is why the label 'Cubist' applied to modern architecture has won little critical favour, and serves only occasionally, and then rather superficially, to explain the code, as Mallet-Stevens would say; it can be more aptly applied to the Classicism of Roux-Spitz or Czech architecture in Prague, which, incidentally, with its turbulent surfaces and intense colourings belongs more to Expressionism. Whereas Cubism aimed at being monochromatic, architecture favoured the prevalence of white, absolutely rejecting the Expressionist fashion for *Fassadenmalerei* (façade painting), which was one of Bruno Taut's strong points.

Nevertheless one cannot deny that there was an aesthetic demand not to be satisfied simply with the formula of rationalism or functionalism, and this can only be ascribed to Cubism. Mallet-Stevens himself moves in that direction under the impetus of his training at the Hoffmann-Schule towards a progressive and aggressive simplification of volumes, the rejection of varied surfaces and overhanging eaves, the breaking up of volumes with angular openings, the splitting up of masses with a masterly mechanism of insets, a *jeu savant* of identically-treated surfaces, all monochrome, without textural vibrations, a direct expression of the concept of an abstract geometric plan. As far back as 1911 he had written: 'Form is the intersection of light and matter.' But his aim in his mature work is for univocal material and immobile light. His effort is directed towards dematerialising architectural language, destructuring the phenomenal and aspiring to the absolute of geometry. But this inclination towards purism is itself a sort of contradiction; as time goes on, geometry resolves itself into a dated language, and this is one of the most pertinent expressions of the 1930s style. Francastel justly pointed out: 'Let us emphasise that it is style, not technique, that has in a most precise way governed the development of modern architecture, not so much from 1890 to 1900, but rather in the period starting from the last years of the nineteenth century, when there appeared the positive doctrine of the machine as a source of beauty, and around 1930 with the theories of useful art. This means that these two periods habitually regarded as fundamental stages in the modern monumental style are generally

Robert Mallet-Stevens (1886–1945): fire-
station at Passy. Preparatory sketch, 1934 and
completed building, 1935.

Robert Mallet-Stevens: design for the interior of the church of St Nicholas, Paris, 1933.

lumped together. Let us also add that this style is linked to Cubism, a term not particularly apt to define a style of painting or sculpture, because one associates it with the entry of a third dimension, time, into the realm of traditional forms, and this is confused with movement.'[5] In this sense the Villa Savoye is more closely linked to Cubism than Duchamp-Villon's Cubist house of 1912.

The Cubist component of 1930s architectural language is not determined so much by the dynamic of movement as by the aesthetic play of volumes, we could even say by their assimilation into the cube and into the parallelepiped of every architectonic element. Take, for example, the famous tub balconies. The balcony, being an overhanging slab, disturbed the Cubist vision, and so was treated as one full volume, like a sarcophagus, and considered as a solid rather than as an empty shape. Only rarely was the slab admitted as an element of transition between the great volumetric cage and the openings of the

E. Sottsass, U. Cuzzi: design for the competition for the renewal of the Via Roma in Turin, 1931.

windows and balconies; the houses by Bassompierre near the Pont Mirabeau in Paris are a lively example.

Our discussion of specific points in the architectural language of the 1930s brings us closer to its constituent elements, and we can now attempt a critical 'zoom-lens' treatment that will hopefully permit a more detailed reading of the themes and problems of the period.

Robert Pommier: building in Place Vauban,
Paris, c.1935.

THE INTEGRALISM OF VOLUMES

Nothing is more irrational than designing architecture in which the walls meet the roof at a sharp-edged right-angle without any transition or overhang of the roof. All the traditional building techniques introduce cornices as a transition, and have the roof overhanging as an umbrella to protect the surface of the façade. But sharp edges were an obsession of the 1930s, and are the reason why modern architecture has aged so prematurely. Some architects adapted themselves to using a 'cover', overhanging or very slightly protruding, or even in a line with the wall but with a recessed transitional section (Victor Bourgeois in the garden-city of Berchem). But the prevailing tendency was for the undisguised meeting of two plain surfaces, the wall and the roof, which naturally could not be of the same material, and thus demanded an artificial means of connection. Likewise, windows, usually horizontal, were simply cut out of the wall brickwork without any cornice or sill, which led to problems of how to drain away rain beating against the recess, which in turn demanded a new solution. Moreover, the problem of the surface itself became technologically tricky. In Italy the rendering known as Terranova was invented; this incorporated colour, was of moderately fine texture, and was thus able to mask the joins, which were otherwise emphasised with fine grooves, or with recessed fillets; this was one possible way of breaking up the surfaces. Another involved the use of the popular grès mosaic, made of little squares two or four centimetres wide, and stuck on like a great sheet of veneer over a prepared surface of crude cement rendering; it offered various colours and textures, clear or opaque, and the pieces were so small that the network of joins hardly showed.

With marble facings, too, a technique was sought that would hide the joins, reduce the sense of thickness, and produce an effect by the use of symmetrical or parallel veining similar to that successfully used for the wood veneers that were at the same time gaining popularity in furniture. A more simple and economical method was fine pebble-dash, inevitably whitewashed in Mediterranean style, or in Italy sometimes painted with strong, would-be Roman ochre, which in the end earned the nickname 'yellow palace'[6] for examples of that unmistakably Fascist architecture. But the problem became more complex where the climate did not favour these simple solutions, and the building industry of Northern Europe produced clinker and brick of more traditional colours which were also much more durable.

The design problem, in fact, centred on the adoption of original solutions for the simple join between roof and wall, between wall and door and window recesses, between wall and balcony and so on. Periodicals such as *Moderne Bauformen* hastened to present constructive ideas, to support the spread of fashionable concepts, and to foster the exchange of experiences. The common requirement was of a strictly formal aesthetic nature; functionalist preaching and the banner of rationality so flaunted concerning the 'distributive character' of architecture gave way suddenly before the demands of a code that, by assuming the geometric model as its base, contradicted the most elementary laws of nature applying to building.

Apartment blocks in Milan: (*top left*) Gio Ponti
and Emilio Lancia: Rasini Tower, Milan,
1933–4. (*bottom left*) Alberto Novello: block
in the Via Melzi d'Eril, Milan, 1930. (*top right*)
Gigiotti Zanini: block in Piazza Duse, Milan.
1933. (*bottom right*) Elio Frizia: block in Piazza
Cinque Giornate, Milan, 1935.

SURFACE TREATED AS A 'PAGE'

Debat-Ponsan: frontage
in the Boulevard
Vaugirard, Paris, c.1930.

As a consequence of reducing the design of the façade to a simple perforated surface stripped of any transitional cornices or contrasting materials, attention turned to the harmony of rectangles within rectangles, to combinations, to symmetry and asymmetry, to continuous bands. Architecture was thus reduced to the state of graphics. The equilibrium of any page is governed by basic laws of proportion, determined by the psychology of vision.

De Stijl and Mondrian in particular had explored the infinite possibilities, the weight and significance involved in the simple insertion of one geometric figure inside another; but the concern of architects was to rationalise the solution, not to entrust it exclusively to intuition, not to consider it as the product of imagination, but as the projection of an intrinsic law governing the harmony of proportion. Wittgenstein had already discussed the significance of 'higher' or 'lower' concerning an opening such as a door, and when it could be called too high, or too low and so on.

The range of acceptability in this matter is really determined by intuitive factors associated with psychology, but not exempt from cultural conditioning – consider the different concepts in the Classical or Renaissance fields, or in the Far East, particularly Japan. Here lies the uncertain boundary between instinct and reason, between the *a priori* almost innate idea of acceptable proportions and the *a posteriori*

Adrien Blomme and Raymond Nicolas: preparatory drawing for the Métropole Cinema in Brussels, 1930, built in 1933.

confirmation of this acceptability. The need to punctuate a façade with continuous or at least extended horizontal apertures came into conflict with the internal division into various areas or dwelling units, so the partitions had to be disguised by the window frames – a solution related, in fact, to the false windows of academicism, had anyone but noticed. This was the exact opposite of Art Nouveau, which was accused of formalism, even though Horta and others felt strongly that openings should advertise the importance of the areas inside. There was also a demand for regrouping, in other words the conjunction of large sheer surfaces contrasted with large windowed surfaces, here too not without detriment to the relationship between exterior and interior and functional restriction. Another problem was how the horizontal window, that key element in the modern architectural language, could relate to others like it. The vertical window, a rectangle in which the base is less than the height, is intrinsically compatible with other equal or similar figures: this is the lesson of history. The horizontal window exhausts its own dynamic, so is a difficult element to couple, triple, or set side by side. It is avoided wherever possible, but even then not without difficulty in relation to interior volumes. It is far easier to adopt large squares or very nearly square rectangles such as are common above all in French architecture, and which are more compatible with the 'cage' concept of reinforced concrete.

(*top and bottom left*) Buildings in Moscow, early 1930s.

(*top centre*) B. Yofan: building in Moscow, 1928–30. (*bottom centre*) Building in the Normalstorg Square in Stockholm, 1934.

(*top right*) Tony Garnier: Town Hall of
Boulogne-Billancourt, 1934. (*bottom right*)
V. Schtiouko and V. Gelfreikh: Rostov Theatre
in Moscow, early 1930s.

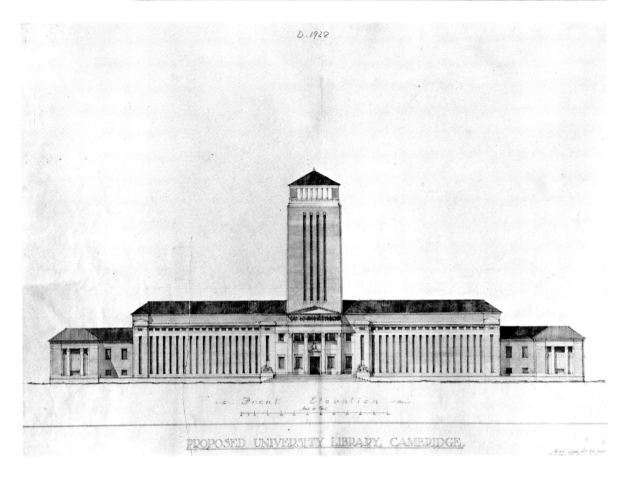

D.1928

Front Elevation

PROPOSED UNIVERSITY LIBRARY, CAMBRIDGE.

Gilbert Scott: front elevation of Cambridge University Library, 1931.

The rationality of the modern, after believing itself rid of all academic trappings, all stylistic demands, and all aesthetic conditions, ran into a fresh series of more subtle restraints, less obvious but no less cogent. The aesthetic tyranny reappeared in association with the simplest elements, such as the adoption of elementary geometric or insistently purist schemes. Rationalism, functionalism, and the new objectivity gave way to this new series of restraints; not that they were really new, it was only that the formal language of past architecture had set them aside, rendering them implicit while formally preserving its liberty. Once all this was eliminated, the problem arose anew, and attention focused again on aesthetic factors, treating their unavoidable importance in a different way.

PROPORTIONS AND REGULATING LINES

'Regulating lines are an insurance against the arbitrary,' declared Le Corbusier in *Vers une architecture*, adding at once: 'The carrying out of inspection sanctions all work created with ardour, like the school-boy's "number you first thought of", the mathematician's QED.' Le Corbusier recognised the value of inspection, post-perfecting, a system of modulating lines consisting of a series of parallel diagonals, similar triangles, or the adoption of the right-angle and the golden section. The search undertaken in *Vers une architecture* (where he apologised for presenting examples from his own works like the Maison Ozenfant because, he wrote, 'in spite of my investigations I have not yet had the pleasure of meeting contemporary architects involved with this question') led to the system of the modular. But Le Corbusier was not to remain alone; Borissavlievitch started in 1926 to compile the history of the theory of proportion; in 1934 Mallet-Stevens designed the cover of his book *Une demeure*, one of the 'Architecture d'aujourd'hui' editions, showing the scheme of the design smothered by a cagework of grids, arcs and triangles governing the essential lines of the building.

By way of reinforcement there is no lack of discordant voices such as Hugo Häring's, who favours organicism and rejects modern proportions. This is why 'the geometric proportions and Classicism are rejected by the modern (but what is its substance, and who incarnates it?) or rather by that modernity represented by the eternal and omni-present formal creative desire, which assumes particular importance as Germanism (it is not a refusal expressed in the name of artistic liberty nor for lack of standards)'.[7] He adds, 'About ten years ago another architect exhorted that architecture be restored; this was Le Corbusier, the modern, when he wrote *Vers une architecture*. Even Le Corbusier has recourse to triangularity; his veneration for geometry is nourished at the same source as Theodor Fischer's. Heir to the Latin culture, Le Corbusier renews the attempt to found on staticity the aesthetic-visual harmony of everyday life with the dissolution of geometrical bodies, injecting vital elements into them in great abundance (but he still remains far behind the dynamism and musicality of German Baroque, because for the Latin architect the operation of dissolving geometry is carried out on a rational, not a figurative basis). Le Corbusier is a classicist who prolongs the Greek, Roman and Renaissance traditions up to our own day, detaching himself from the modern tendency to postulate building as an organism.'[8]

The use of regulating lines spread, and there was a revival in the popularity of the theory of proportions such as had not been seen since the Renaissance. What did all this mean? We have already seen how it was the product of a sort of vertigo brought on by the emptiness of shapes, as if rationality transferred into the area of aesthetics offered itself as a system in which to inscribe every product of the imagination, as if freedom had need of standards, as if with the substitution of geometry for the 'rule of the orders' there came to the fore a new system of rules – or rather an ancient one, that affected harmony, rendering it accessible, recognisable, reproduceable. The relationship between standards and freedom, a recurrent argument in every

Hans Poelzig (1869–1936): design for the new Reichshauptbank in Berlin, 1932. *Opposite*: design for the new Reichshauptbank in Berlin, 1932. Ground-floor plan.

creation of art and particularly architecture, again became dramatically evident.

But the reintroduction of a system of standards also provided an opportunity to transgress them. The first condition of the classic system of harmony is that it is self-contained, producing balance and resulting in the closed form, and the simplest way to achieve this is through symmetry. By contrast, asymmetry became strongly attractive, offering dynamism and openness of form; the most immediate means available was that of 'repetition', the insistent reintroduction of an element whose constant appearance gave rise to rhythm. From Le Corbusier onwards, eurhythmics became the centre of attention. Already the reference to Gothic had served to reintroduce the element of repetition; it was now to become obsessive and military in Nazi architecture, and, like the goose-step, it was a particularly German phenomenon. Repetition is the opposite of variation, a form of insurance against the casual, and one of the safest ingredients of monumentality. There is nothing like it in nature; repetition is inherent in the fixed number to the point of belying it and losing all sense of odd and even. Three, five, seven – the canonic numbers of repetition in architecture – are replaced by the number n; from indeterminate to indeterminate implies dynamism and open form.

There was yet another element introduced into the language of the 1930s as a kind of modern transgression, and that was distortion. The fine arts had taught the expressive value of distortion applied to realism, had stressed the factor of exaggeration in Picasso's classical women and certain twentieth-century sculpture, and had reintroduced vertical distortion not without reference to the taste of the

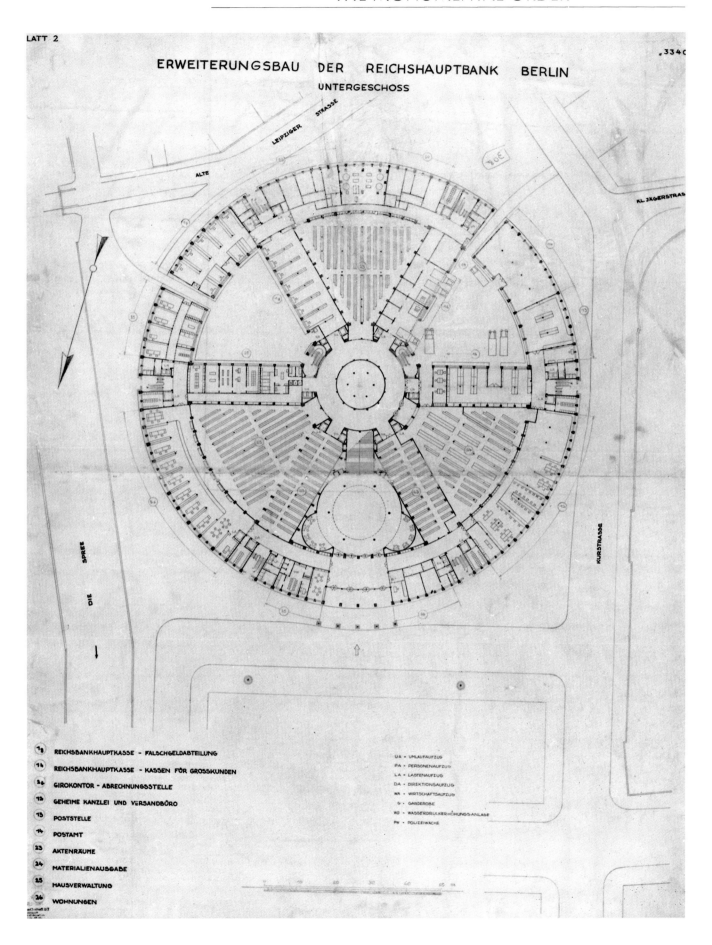

LATT 2

ERWEITERUNGSBAU DER REICHSHAUPTBANK BERLIN
UNTERGESCHOSS

1a REICHSBANKHAUPTKASSE - FALSCHGELDABTEILUNG
1b REICHSBANKHAUPTKASSE - KASSEN FÜR GROSSKUNDEN
2a GIROKONTOR - ABRECHNUNGSSTELLE
12 GEHEIME KANZLEI UND VERSANDBÜRO
13 POSTSTELLE
14 POSTAMT
23 AKTENRÄUME
24 MATERIALIENAUSGABE
25 HAUSVERWALTUNG
26 WOHNUNGEN

UA = UMLAUFAUFZUG
PA = PERSONENAUFZUG
LA = LASTENAUFZUG
DA = DIREKTIONSAUFZUG
WA = WIRTSCHAFTSAUFZUG
G = GARDEROBE
WD = WASSERDRUCKERHÖHUNGSANLAGE
PW = POLIZEIWACHE

Sir Edwin Lutyens: design for the headquarters
of Reuters news agency at 85 Fleet Street (main
elevation), London, 1935.

Paul Tournon and
Marcel Chappey:
competition design for
the OTUA, Paris, 1934.

primitives and Gothic architecture's columnar statues. Vertical elongation is a sign of the way shapes tend to become architectural, to which Focillon drew attention in *La vie des formes*, next to Valéry's *Eupalinos*, one of this period's basic texts on aesthetics.

Vertical elongation is one of the components of 1930s architectural language that transgresses Classicism while still conserving certain elements and reminders of it, and it is also one of the factors in the sought-after monumentality. Verticalism, symbolising the ambition to conquer static compatibilities, is a factor in monumentality because it dehumanises proportions, breaking the anthropomorphic equilibrium of Renaissance Classicism. A possible though improbable element of reconciliation between Classical and Gothic, verticalism constitutes an ineradicable factor of modernism because it accentuates its rational, cephalocratic significance, removing all hint of naturalism and all organic reference. To paraphrase Wittgenstein, 'too high' is a judgement that implies an instinctive notion of the correct height founded on ancestral memories and a subconscious cultural assimilation of Classical models. 'Never too high' is an assertion of violence, a reconquest of freedom, an ambition to exceed a subconscious limit. Repetition and vertical distortion are the ingredients of a new monumentality, an opportunity to transgress Classicism, an affirmation of the 'modern' as an open work, breaking away from historical equilibrium.

(*above*) Giuseppe de Finetti: design for the
reconstruction of Milan city centre, 1934.
(*below*) A. Schtoussev: design for residential
block on the Rostov Quay, Moscow, 1938.

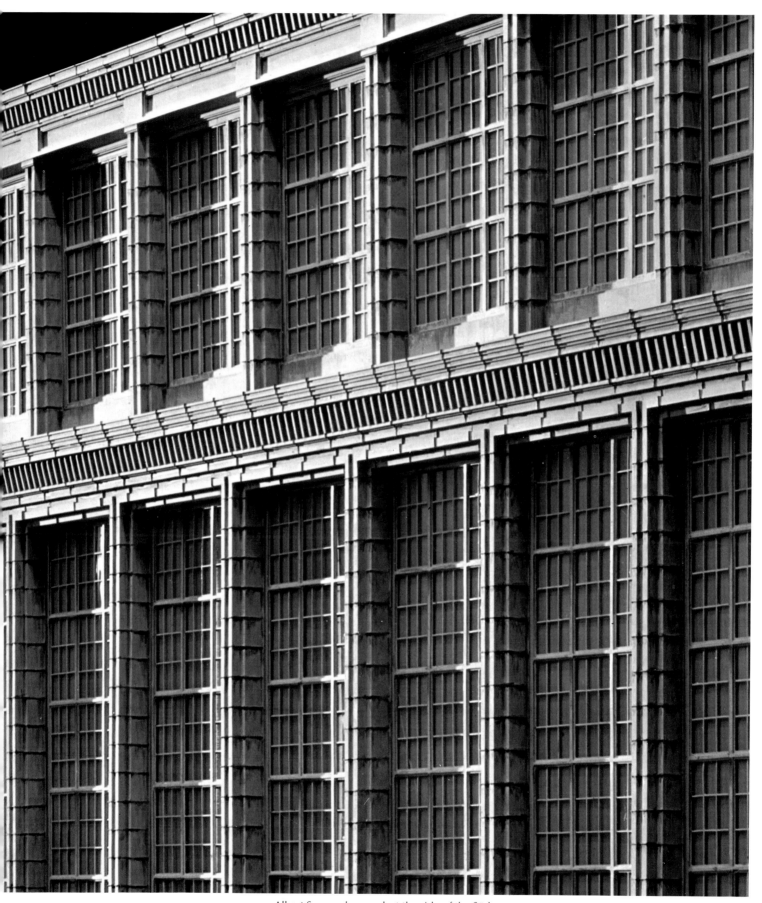

Albert Speer: glass-work at the side of the Süd-
Bahnhof, Berlin, 1939.

NATIONAL SPIRIT

Analysis of the architectural language of the 1930s leads to the identification of certain common themes and problems, but this does not imply the exclusion of those intensely national characteristics reflecting political nationalism, which was particularly strong in this period, and each nation's own historical character and inherent nature. Although these were especially highlighted by the dictatorships, who glorified the distinction of race, they were no less discernible in the democracies too. One result of the Depression following the Wall Street Crash was the prevalence of public commissions over private. These public commissions tended to accentuate nationalistic characteristics, since the client was directly committed to expressing political and ideological convictions through architecture.

The contemporary history of architecture concentrates on the formation of the international style – according to CIAM – and identifies this with progress itself, equating it with deliverance from the distress of a restrictive political policy, or even dictatorship, as in Italy. But national spirit persists as one of the most significant elements, not so much in the results themselves, the architectural products, but in the method, the overall mentality, the very conception of the architect's profession, the hypothesis of a modern architectural language not completely divorced from tradition. It is not easy to distinguish between Swedish, German, Czech, Belgian, Dutch, English, French and Italian architecture, nor can their national characteristics be outlined without recourse to dangerous schematisation. In reality the dialectic between international and national styles was an intermediate dialectic; the former was suspected of Bolshevism – probably by analogy with the Socialist International and the Cominform – even though this was denied by the Soviets. The international style was seen as an expression of Jewish economic power, condemned as 'foreign', and apparently resisted everywhere, both by political ideologists and, in a more subtle and concrete way, by the bodies responsible for approving plans and public administration in general.

The outcome of this dialectic should not be evaluated only as a clash between radical elements and the forces of conservative inertia, otherwise there is a risk of a teleological interpretation of history, one of the more recurrent forms of deviation from historical accuracy; even if true objectivity is unattainable, the complexity of the elements concerned should never be lost sight of. Therefore at this point it is essential to try to delineate the aspects of what may be called *national spirit*, meaning the specific contribution that each nation brought to the debate, the architectural production, and the design of this period.

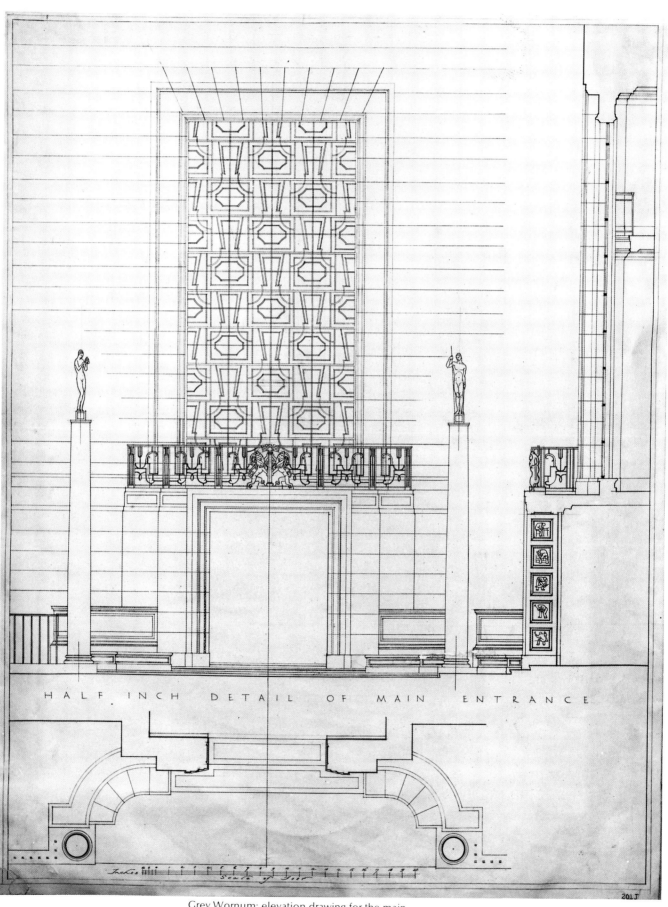

HALF INCH DETAIL OF MAIN ENTRANCE

Grey Wornum: elevation drawing for the main
entrance of the headquarters of the RIBA,
Portland Place, London, 1934.

Iarijan Ivacci: Jugoslav pavilion at the Paris
International Exhibition, 1937.

Two watercolour drawings by English
architects, 1932: (above) E.V. Harris, City Hall,
Sheffield. (below) Giles Gilbert Scott: design
for a house.

ENGLAND

England is characterised by an abundance of images that reflect its democratic way of life, its open door to refugees, and the profound transformation brought about by the 1929 crisis and its economic and social consequences.

In 1936 fire destroyed the Crystal Palace, symbol of nineteenth-century progress and spread of Empire – that same Empire which Gandhi with his campaign of civil disobedience was now beginning to shake to its foundations. Le Corbusier's *Vers une architecture* was translated in 1927 and exercised its 'incantatory fervour'.[1] The Dutchman Willem Dudok was awarded the RIBA gold medal, and exercised his influence with his famous Hilversum Town Hall. In 1934 Walter Gropius arrived in England and worked for several years with Maxwell Fry. There was also a Russian element; Berthold Lubetkin of the Tecton Group, born at Tbilisi in Georgia, arrived in 1930, a few years after Serge Chermayeff, a Caucasian, on his way like everyone to the United States, and a colleague of Eric Mendelsohn.

From 1933 to 1936 London was a staging-post for refugee intellectuals and subsequently a refuge for governments in exile. This led to singular openmindedness towards modernism, regarded suspiciously by traditionalists as 'continental' or 'bolshie'. An upholder of tradition, Sir Reginald Blomfield, proclaimed, 'Since the war modernism, or modernismus as it should be called on the German precedent, has invaded this country like an epidemic, and though there are signs of reaction its attack is insidious and far-reaching, with the wholly fallacious prospect of a new heaven and a new hearth which it dangles before the younger generation.'[2] But the argument did not provoke a verbal explosion, and no ideological clash came about. With their natural empiricism the English quelled the argument with a simple recipe, typology, from which not even recent publications have escaped, and which possessed the undeniable merit of a splendid sense of opportunity, judging by the 'Thirties' Exhibition held in 1979 at the Hayward Gallery, London.

From the country house and the traditional cottage, each in its own way, emerged the idea of the modern house; the example of the house that Gropius built for himself was seminal, as was the model of Le Corbusier's Villa Savoye. But at the same time a robust eclectic historicist tradition survived, of which the most successful exponent in the early years of the century was Sir Edwin Lutyens, who also realised a notable output in this decade too, aside from his work in India, Spain and South Africa. He was never remotely deflected by the modern style. Between 1895, when he produced his first designs, and 1944, when he was already thinking about the rebuilding of London, he let Art Nouveau, Expressionism, Neue Sachlichkeit, Rationalism, Functionalism and Organicism pass him by unmoved, nor did he experience a moment's doubt that by drawing on Norman Shaw, Webb, Butterfield, Vanbrugh, Hawksmoor, Wren and Palladio there was enough to meet all the demands of the self-made man's commissions, and please the readers of *Country Life*, which was the journal in which he chose to publish, though it is not, of course, primarily an architectural journal. Between Oliver Hill and Lutyens there is room for what has been defined as the dynamics of 'traditional versus modern' (an expression already couched in terms of the Modern Movement, and probably better replaced by 'the pluralism of private concerns'). Certainly other types of buildings are 'modern', starting with the famous *Daily Telegraph* and *Daily Express* buildings, which between 1928 and 1931 introduced into Fleet Street an aggressive interpretation of modernity condemned at the time as a 'pretentious mixture of neo-graeco-egyptian'; in addition there were the radio headquarters, cinemas, sports centres, seaside resorts and airports. Builders discovered the advantage of the multi-storey block of modern flats, on which, in addition to the poetic and highly practical design of the Penguin House at the London Zoo, the fortunes of the Tecton Group were based.

In the building of City Halls there was a tussle between the influence of Dudok and a robust traditional Classicism, in churches between some suggestion of teutonic modernism and a consolidated furtherance of the neo-medieval. In buildings for industry and transport there prevailed a kind of monumental industrial rhetoric, remotely derived from Behrens, culminating in the chimney columns of Gilbert Scott's Battersea Power Station. But when the RIBA celebrated its centenary in 1934 by building a new headquarters designed by Grey Wornum in Portland Place, it chose a monumental language which reintroduced neo-Georgian qualities in a rhetorical and traditionalist key, offering an alternative trend to rationalism. Proto-rationalist in fact, it related to a chic, 'class' vision of London architecture, which constitutes a further interesting aspect of the blend of traditional continuity and modern style in British architecture. The language of the 1930s was also employed in the great complex of public buildings commissioned by London University in Bloomsbury, with its famous Library Tower in Portland stone, and that of Adastral House, and of great commercial and diplomatic buildings, such as Australia House. Mendelsohn's modern style inspired certain large stores such as Simpson's of Piccadilly, and the lobby décor of a number of important hotels such as the Cumberland and the Strand Palace though without ever being permitted to appear outside!

Neo-Georgian, international style and eclectic historicism intermix in this way, according to typological divisions, not rigid, but with just that suggestion of ritualism typical of the behaviour of English society, which always respectfully admits revolutionary voices to the system when they proceed from an affirmation of individuality rather than adherence to a trend. Although the architect's profession may have been reorientated towards the public sector, towards government and bureaucracy, the conception of its 'artistic' nature remains assured; witness the high standard of its design drawings, and the continuance of great artists' impressions as a form of collective communication and persuasion. The use of traditional techniques, mainly watercolour, for the presentation of designs, is to a great extent reassuring. It seems to make the modern language acceptable and guarantee its aesthetic intentions.

Giles Gilbert Scott and Theodore Holliday:
Battersea Power Station, London, 1931.

Charles Holden: design
for the University of
London (watercolour),
1933.

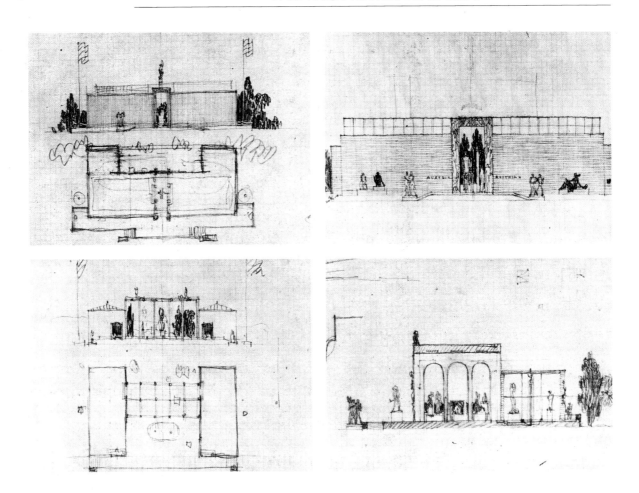

Josef Hoffmann (1870–1956): four studies for the Austrian pavilion at the Venice Biennale, 1934.

GERMANY AND AUSTRIA

The interpretation of the German scene in the 1930s can be considered under several headings. The first is concerned with the development of Nazi architecture, the exodus of refugee architects, the discrediting of the Modern Movement, the Bauhaus (whose importance has perhaps been exaggerated as far as its influence in Germany itself is concerned). The second relates to industrial buildings which drew on structuralist-rationalist ideas for strictly functional reasons. Finally, there was the encouragement of regional vernacular, whose ideological precedents were a lot older than Nazism. It is only much later that the contemporary history of architecture has cast light on the Expressionist movement, on the profoundly innovative influence that this exerted before the First World War and its utopian and imaginative consequences from the point of view of 'objectivity' and 'expression', two qualities suppressed by rationalist formalism. How did the demands and the imaginative peaks derived from Expressionism during the war, the defeat and the period of inflation come to an end, to be reconciled with the reality of the reconstruction work and housing policy of the Weimar Republic, in which Taut himself, the brains of the Ring,[3] had become one of the leading figures? This is also a story that has been explored both in the technological construction sense, and in the context of urban and residential developments – areas in which Germany was in the lead over the rest of Europe.

Emil Fahrenkamp (1885–1966): Rhenania
Haus, Berlin, 1932. Model and finished
building.

105

Hans Poelzig: (*above*) design for the
Schauburg, 1932. Interior. (*below*) Competition
design for the monument 'To the glory of the
Reich', 1932.

Hans Poelzig: Offices of
I.G. Farben, Frankfurt,
1928–1930.

But between Nazism, Expressionism and *Heimatstil*, the history
of contemporary architecture seems to have left in the shade figures
such as Poelzig, Hagen, Schumacher, Fahrenkamp, Bonatz, Böhm,
Schweizer, Hertlein, Issel, and many more whose works are documented in journals of the period and who constitute a trend
independent of Nazism, though without giving rise to the Party's dis-
pleasure. 'Today,' wrote Poelzig, 'we almost go so far as to hail the
discovery of a new style when water no longer floods the cellars, in
other words when the basic problems of building technique have
been satisfactorily solved. For the moment we have shelved the
stylistic question and are trying to reconstruct from scratch the
technical basis of building according to the present level of development of technology.'[4]

A common and characteristic concern is with the 'probity' of
building: expressive themes are proposed, useless formalism is
rejected as are suggestions which are intrinsically about building
technique itself. Poelzig adds, virtually autobiographically, since it
reflects the course of his own experience, 'The road towards present-
day architecture set out from the reform of industrial building. We
older ones, who a generation ago threw ourselves into industrial
architecture, had at that time a real craving to work in a field that was
not yet cultivated, and in which there reigned no predetermined
habits of historical style . . . Every attempt to break in failed, and only in
industrial architecture did we encounter less resistance.'[5]

Another element – having a certain continuity with Bismarck's
Germany – is the quest for monumentality, a kind of Nietzschean

desire for power applied not only to strictly industrial buildings but also to commercial and financial ones and offices in urban environments; a desire to depict Germany as concerned with method, clarity of mind, technique, seriousness and commitment to work, far from its experiences of power, defeat, the unfair Treaty of Versailles, the disintegration of the *putsch* period and inflation; a Germany in which the road to Bolshevism had at last been barred, and in which the economic forces presented themselves as – and soon proved to be – a power with which the mounting tide of Nazism would have to reckon.

A further element belongs to German architectural thought in the twentieth century, whether pre-Nazi or extra-Nazi. This is the capacity to select a theme, even to the extent of being obsessed with a particular theme. To quote Poelzig again, 'Liebermann says that "painting is deciding what to leave out!". In modern architecture we have now arrived at the same point, whereas before "designing architecture" nearly always meant adding in excess.'[6] Leaving out is not only simplifying but choosing, concentrating on the essential, giving each building a dominant theme – Fahrenkamp's Shell Haus springs to mind immediately – which, as already observed, by means of the technique of repetition achieves a monumental effect, giving to each building a distinctive appearance which becomes a symbol for the clients themselves. It is a way of treating each piece of architecture as a fresh entity, instead of applying a cipher or predictable formula. It is these elements – technical and construction factors, the choice of a single theme, the symbolic value which follows – which constitute the 'eloquence' of the modern German 1930s style prior to the Nazi 'rhetoric'; the ingredients are extremely simple from an intellectual point of view, even if they had to reckon with the by then established reliability of construction technique, which was to lead, as already observed, in the case of certain schemes to a mythical search for 'durability'. Never in the history of architecture was there such a desire for durability with such ephemeral results.

Very different is the Austrian contribution, which involves greater modesty and refinement, almost a kind of romantic aestheticism. Not only did Hoffmann develop his particular language undaunted, he applied it to works which became representative of the Austrian style, such as the pavilion at the Venice Biennale. But while the Hoffmann-schule was responsible for spreading the master's formal approach, the Wiener Werkstätte, before its crisis, became responsible for more and more that was escapist and fantastic. Under the influence of Czeschka, they churned out the popular idiom. The figure who best represents the Modern Movement was Josef Frank, who has been virtually ignored until recent reappraisals. The Austrian architect who tackled his assignments in terms of modern Classicism was Holzmeister, who carried out his work in Turkey, where it became representative of Atatürk's republic.

(*above*) Emil Fahrenkamp: German house at
the International Water Exhibition, Liège,
1932. (*below*) Josef Hoffmann: Austrian
pavilion at the Venice Biennale, 1934.

Georges Gori: *The Spirit of Fascism* outside the
Italian pavilion at the Paris International
Exhibition, 1937.

ITALY

In Italy, where argument and loquacity are endogenous, the verbal quest for a national style echoed from every quarter. Rationalism was accused of being xenophilic, pro-German or pro-Nordic, while Futurism's claims to being Italian and original were counterpoised by the indigenous roots – Roman in fact – of rationalist architecture. Emphasis was placed on the Latin spirit and the Italian tendency. As far back as 1923, Roberto Papini had written, 'Italian art, pure expression of the normal equilibrium of the race, has always magnificently maintained the halfway position between the Nordic currents engrossed in decorating the truth, and the oriental currents all pervaded with sensual arabesques and intoxicated with colour.'[7] And in 1932, passing from the decorative arts to architecture, Papini write 'Forms from beyond the Alps are far from fully accepted; anything dry, rigid and mechanical in German architecture is refused, anything decorative or affected in French architecture is banished.'[8] And the architects of Gruppo 7 proclaimed, 'From the monumental edifice to the cover of a book, Germany and Austria possess one style. This style, more solid in Germany, perhaps more refined and precious in Austria, has a very definite personality. You either like it or not, but you cannot ignore it. Moreover it has a markedly nationalistic character, and this should be reason enough, even if there were no other, to show how wrong they were who thought they could renew Italian architecture by transplanting German fashions, perfectly respectable of course, but out of place among us.'[9] The *excusatio non petita* of internationalism, which should have been a welcome feature considering the provincialism with which Italian culture was struggling, was immediately shrugged off, or at least an attempt was made to shrug off the influence, on all occasions and by every writer, until Rava in 1931, in an article in *Domus* pointedly entitled 'Dangerous turning', suggested, 'Of course we know that the best of Italian rationalists are assisted by an alert sense of discrimination; we know that before they accept and use any element or form that ranks as having *international* value, being universally adopted as the result of the combined searches and experiments of European rationalists, they evaluate it with particular care also from the aesthetic angle, and judge it with a classic sense of balance and proportion; but this is not and cannot be enough. We wish that when faced even with the best works of foreign rationalism Italians would assume the attitude that one of Paul Morand's characters attributes to French intellectual inclination, when he says, "Le goût français n'est pas de dire oui mais de dire non" ("The French inclination is to reject rather than accept"). We wish in fact that they would not remain satisfied by the best and most refined of foreign elements. We wish instead that on the basis, granted, of their experience of the most true and vital rationalism and of the already universal elements it has imposed, Italian architects would feel the need to create according to their own race, their own culture, and their own personality.'[10]

This led to the attempt to associate Modernism with Fascism and to the crude affirmations of the *Manifesto for rational architecture* delivered to Mussolini on the occasion of the second MIAR exhibition in Rome in March 1931,[11] such as, 'The architecture of Mussolini's era must reflect the masculinity, the force and the pride of the revolution. The old architects are emblems of an impotence that does not suit us.' And again, 'Our movement has no other moral charge than to serve the Revolution in this hard climate.'[12] The Italian architectural controversy fell apart in the midst of this sort of sycophancy towards the ambiguities of the régime, and sank to the banal, 'He spoke ill of Garibaldi!' when tradition was offended, or making fun of those who, as Belli[13] put it, waved 'a shred of Roman toga' in tradition's name. Apart from the debate between 'moderate' and 'radical' there was an insistent nationalist anti-German tone, which coincided with Mussolini's policy in his anti-Hitler phase, when he sent a division to defend Austria at the Brenner Pass. 'Specific Nordic and Teutonic traits are absoluteness and therefore unilaterality,' wrote Plinio Marconi in 1933. 'An excess of will-power, under-articulated and ill-directed, which implies going immediately to the limit in everything, forgetting to work in the field of intermediate reality . . . Dominant in the Italic spirit, however, is balance, the ability to synthesise, the capacity to combine the most disparate elements of life into a higher unity; this means to operate completely within the bounds of reality, not to forget any element of life, but to encompass them all within a harmony that may be articulate and complex, but is at the same time perfectly clear.'[14]

There was also the nationalistic aspiration according to Piacentini with his *Defence of Italian Architecture*, published in 1931 and available throughout Europe. Against Gropius and Mendelsohn, who were accused of 'Hebrewism' and internationalism, he suggested Holland and France as models. 'The older nations, the Flemish and French, rich like the Italians with great art traditions, have sensed imperiously this appeal of the spirit of the race,'[15] while, he goes on to suggest, nations with minor artistic traditions, or none at all, like the Czechs and the Jugoslavs, have adhered unreservedly to international trends. 'Even in Germany,' adds Piacentini, 'some very young talents (schools of Fahrenkamp) are already seeking their own personal imprint making use of all the technical achievements and thus creating modern work of great refinement, but freely, with genius and imagination, without deliberately sacrificing the beauty and durability of materials or renouncing expressivity or emotions.'[16]

Banality reaches a high point in the debate between Ojetti and Piacentini on the question of the arch and the column, stuffed with historical lists, always invoking the principle of authority, so that neither of them should lose the favour of the one authority that counted – the Duce; he must really have been amused at this skirmish, while he slyly and cunningly granted his favours to opposing camps, according to the chameleon-like quality which allowed the régime simultaneously to isolate and cultivate the hardliners of *squadrismo*[17] and society circles, while at the same time supporting bourgeois arguments.

If there really was a specific Italian contribution to the language of the 1930s in terms of the nationalism which constitutes one of the recurring themes of the period, it is not to be found in the poverty of debate nor in the verbal fencing, but in certain urban proposals, in a

A. Libera: competition design for the Rome
auditorium, 1935.

(*above*) L. Moretti:
competition design for
the Palazzo della Civiltà
Italiana at E'42. (*below*)
Giovanni Muzio: design
for the building of Il
Popolo d'Italia, Milan.

desire to create an atmosphere of magical realism akin to a religion of 'mystery' such as Bontempelli aspired to with his vision of the city as a unity, and which led him to say, 'Already the notion of a city plan is being established as a fitting subject for architecture. Modern architecture cannot consider itself as other than city architecture. Architecture is coming to assume *an almost narrative look.*'[18] The image and, so to speak, the poetry of the city were rivalled by both the iconoclastic dynamism of the Futurists and by the frozen, contemplative air, the silent noon of the Metaphysicists.

In fact, in the absence of an unequivocal directive from the régime (contrast this with the Nazis, or later the Phalangists) not every Italian architect was involved in the debate between lovers of the past and rationalists, between moderates and radicals, between internationalists and nationalists and so forth; but in the north, principally in Milan, perhaps because of its relative autonomy, its detachment and the sometimes ostentatious xenophilia on the part of local government and industry, there was a highly professional standard of independent work – involving Muzio, Ponti, Lancia, Portaluppi, Ulrich and others. This was responsible for developing a Neoclassical image of Milan in the 1930s which conferred on the city a truly European dimension.

Milan thus succeeded in creating an environment that affected the city and the decorative arts, a seat of culture, with the journals *Domus*, *Casabella* and *Stile*, and the Triennale. It became the moral capital of modern architecture. It gave the lie to the vulgar criticism that identified as Fascist all architecture not properly rationalist and modern, demonstrating the same pluralism of attitude that, in spite of the obligatory acts of homage, of the *captatio benevolentiae*, really did align itself with the complexity and contradictions of contemporary European architecture

In Rome the situation was different; since its establishment as the national capital following the unification of Italy, architecture there had always had problems of reconciling conflicting roles: the architecture required of a capital city, the architecture of renewal, and the monumental architecture linked to Fascism. There were also authentic local trends, as in the work of Aschieri, whose theatrical, post-Expressionist compositions achieved a rare efficacy, the continuation of the Barocchetto line with Fasolo and Foschini, the aggressive formalism which characterised the trio Ridolfi, Moretti and Libera – modernists but certainly not rationalists – and the Pompeiian nostalgia of Del Debbio and the Foro Italico. In all a season here too not without some happy episodes, at a time when the new cities of the Pontine Marshes were getting under way, and there was the rhetorical and Utopian prospect of E'42.

If one seeks a specific Italian quality in 1930s architecture it is to be found not in the realm of ideas and cultural debate, nor in the town-planning operations in ancient cities such as Turin, Genoa, Bergamo, Brescia, Trieste, Bolzano and the like, but rather in certain urban fragments and single works of architecture, where unselfconscious poetry wedded to creativity succeeded in producing a series of 'pseudoconcepts' which sometimes even became transferred to titles of slim journals such as *Arte Mediterranea* or *Aria d'Italia*. Apart from this, the Modern Movement was confined to rural villages and the third class of transatlantic liners, while architects, particularly those with metropolitan ambitions, did not lose sight of European values.

(*above*) Gigiotti Zanini: entry hall in a building in the Piazza Duse, Milan, 1933–1934. (*below*) Antonio Bordoni, Luigi Maria Caneva, Antonio Carminati: Trade Union Building, Corso di Porta Vittoria, Milan, 1930–1932.

(*above*) Giovanni Muzio: Palazzo dell'Arte, Viale Alemagna, Milan, 1933. (*below, left to right*) Aldo Andreani: Palazzo Fidia, Via Melegari, Milan, 1924–1930 — Piero Portallupi: building on the Via Giorgio Jan, Milan, 1929 — Aldo Andreani: building on the Via Serbelloni, Milan, 1924–1930.

BELGIUM

The situation in Belgium is unusually complex because it reflects all the contradictions of the decade of the 1930s. Belgium fell into step with modern Europe and produced great works like the tunnel under the Scheldt (1932), a pioneering example of urban planning on several levels, and the Albert Canal (1939) between Antwerp and Liège, connecting the twin souls of Belgian culture, the Flemish and the Walloon. In addition, the international exhibitions at Antwerp and Liège in 1930 and Brussels in 1935 constituted a shop window, a network for cultural exchanges, in spite of the economic crisis.

The principles had already been established in the preceding decade; in the catalogue of the 1973 London and Brussels exhibition, a passage by Delevoy splendidly sums up the prevailing logic: 'This astonishing production, marked by the technology of a fully developed industrial society, was subject in principle to pressure from liberals and technocrats alike. In fact, however natural it seems to us today to see it as part of the international modernist trend of the period, it was a style of architecture that produced images unexpected by the ruling bourgeoisie, who were intellectual, progressive and technocratic. But they accepted them for what they were with evident satisfaction (the satisfaction of participating actively in a reorganisation of their way of life, occupying new spaces, benefitting from domestic developments inspired by a smart functionalist code, and favouring the absolute reduction of form to function) without becoming aware of the alienation concealed within the images in question, without suspecting the circumstantial incongruities that elements belonging to privileged groups threw in front of these boxes, these unusual or secretly aggressive objects: because during the decade 1920–1930 they revived an image of a superseded style, the image of the 1900s (represented in Belgium by the architecture of Victor Horta). I find it sociologically interesting to observe the phenomenon that this same image was to some extent contested as early as 1905–1910 by that other bourgeoisie of merchants and industrialists who, after having patronised, financed and supported Art Nouveau, abandoned their exciting urban properties in Brussels and took over the surrounding countryside, where they erected peaceful 'villas' or 'châteaux' specially designed in academic terms to marry the hallmarks of Gothic and Renaissance and at the same time mark the withdrawal it was necessary to make before the extension, proliferation and socialisation of Art Nouveau and its appropriation by a middle class from whom they wished to keep their distance.'[19]

Thus we observe a proliferation of modern architecture: De Koninck, Bourgeois, Hoste, Braem and others developed rational-functional architecture, based on the teaching of Le Corbusier, an architecture that evinced the desire to make statements, always a feature of the liberal-bourgeois world of Belgium.

Things were different when there was an attempt to bring the language of modern architecture into the public orbit, and here we see the belated employment of Art Nouveau masters. Horta, with his usual talent for environmental aptness, realised an example of Art Deco monumentality with his Palais des Beaux-Arts of 1928, where he

Competition for the Royal Albertine Library,
Brussels, 1937. (*above*) Design by René Braem.
(*below*) Anonymous design.

(*above*) Jean Deligne: entrance to the Rémy
factory at Wygmael, 1930. (*below*) Van de
Velde: Library tower at the University of Ghent,
1935–1939.

abandoned iron and tried out the sinuous language of reinforced concrete. Then in the Central Station, designed in collaboration with Brunfaut, he employed the language of the 1930s, although in the concave-convex interplay of the façade he echoed his old preferences from the Maison du Peuple. As chairman of the jury which judged the competition for the United Nations Headquarters in Geneva, Horta is to be blamed for the traditionalist and eclectic choice and the rejection of Le Corbusier's design. When Horta was made a baron he displayed the typical reflex of a great notable of Belgian architectural culture; he left his studio house, the masterpiece he had built for himself in the Rue Americaine and moved to the more socially rewarding address of the Avenue Louise. Relations with Van de Velde were deadly, and there is evidence in Horta's unpublished memoirs of really quite malign feelings towards his rival, particularly regarding his stay in Switzerland during the 1914–18 war, even insinuating that he was guilty of spying for the Germans. In 1936 Van de Velde built the Central Library at the University of Ghent. Its famous, monumentally modernistic tower confirms his great facility for moving with the times, and indeed he witnessed from the turn of the century onwards all the unrest and the opportunities that the twentieth century was to bring.

In addition to these few works, and after the long gestation period of the Central Station (which was in effect more Brunfaut's work than Horta's), public architecture tackled matters associated with the reconstruction of the capital city and its official 'face' in a situation of considerable uncertainty. Unlike neighbouring Holland, where the Amsterdam school, independently of Berlage's influence, had discovered a vein of genius and forged its own language, Belgium was exposed to French influence, above all in town planning, and was to witness the most sweeping attempts at planning, which attacked even the precious historic fabric of Brussels and Antwerp. Antwerp was the target, in 1933, on the occasion of the competition for the *rive gauche*, of a design for a *ville radieuse* realised with the collaboration of Le Corbusier and the Belgians Hoste and Loquet.

On the other hand, the historicist language did not have the permanent institutional force of the French Beaux-Arts tradition. Art Nouveau had been absorbed since the end of the previous decade, and its widespread success had put paid to the institutionality of Classicism; possible traces of monumentality can be sought within a modern architectural language now affected by Dutch influences, as in the house built in 1930 by Jean Ramekers in the Avenue Molière, or in the simplified, almost Nazi symmetry of the Festival Hall and the Remy factory welfare centre of 1933 by Jean Deligne; two years later the latter also designed a glass box of the modern type as an exhibition pavilion for the same industry. These various influences were found in the most unusual juxtaposition with 1930s monumentality, as in the Royal Albertine Library of 1935 that René Braem designed in strict symmetry, with surfaces given uniformity by means of distempering which made use of a spraying technique (a technique which had great success in Italy too at that time, along with bold drawings made with a graphite stick, in a kind of tribute to Pompeii). In other works of his, such as the design for Brussels Central Station, or in his town-planning proposals, or later in his post-World War Two buildings in Antwerp,

Victor Horta:
competition design for
the Gare centrale,
Brussels, 1940.

Braem could be considered allied to the Modern Movement.

The notion of 'surrender to modernism' which characterises the whole of contemporary architectural historiography does not yield sufficient documentation; the admirable Archives d'Architecture moderne,[20] taking into account the lack of reliable information concerning the situation in Belgium, were the first to propose the collection of further data, and even they have had to begin by trying to evaluate as far as possible the quality of Belgian culture and the liveliness of a debate which has tended to be eclipsed by developments in Europe in general or the architectural fame of neighbouring Holland. But Belgium, even though faithful to its democratic traditions, even though not contaminated by dictatorship, was no less alive than the rest of Europe to the question of the monumental order, and the areas of endeavour were those urban situations in which the conventions of bourgeois architecture no longer sufficed; there, wedged between France and Germany, Belgium was trying to find itself.

A. and Y. Blomme:
design for the Gare du
Midi and its approach,
Brussels, 1936.

HOLLAND: THE 'NIEUWE BOUWEN' DYKE BREACHED BY CLASSICISM

The problems posed by a reconsideration of modern architecture throughout Europe prove even more difficult in the case of Holland, the country generally considered as most favoured by the development of the Modern Movement. Nor can any sort of continuity in terms of Classicism be perceived beyond the examples natural to a country which, as a great port, was open to a variety of styles and influences, from Mannerism to Gothic and French Classicism. Holland contributes, if anything, its own emotive, figurative quality accompanied by structural organisation and geometry; these are features which characterise Dutch painting with its rarefied image of architecture culminating in the surrealistic realism of Saenredam and the abstract geometric elements of the historical avant-garde and the De Stijl group.

But historiographic convention is determined to regard Holland's internal debate only as crisis, recession and 'surrender', in which the influence of a Nazi minority on the political plane is certainly not a crucial element. 'The crisis was due to the Nationalist policy which led in Germany to opposition against progressive thought and the closure of the Bauhaus in 1933. In Holland, Nazism increased in importance relative to the main Liberal-Protestant, Catholic and Socialist parties (from 1930 to 1940).'[21]

An explanation can, perhaps, be sought in the formal and monumental qualities inherent in Hendrik Berlage and in the complex language of the Amsterdam school, dense with plastic qualities, Expressionist feeling, symbolic presences and intense textural qualities, which were to be purified but also castrated in rationalism and the CIAM formula. But this is a different matter, mentioned here only to suggest it is worth looking into.

The documents so painstakingly traced by Fanelli,[22] however, permit the internal debate to be reconstructed, if we ignore his rather solemn judgements and set aside his convictions which are generally allied to the modernist position. The debate began in 1932 when the major affirmation of Functionalism coincided with the crisis of the rejection of its principles by Group 32. This was a group of young artists mainly from Amsterdam or the Haarlem school who gathered round Arthur Staal; although Staal sided with 'the myth of the machine', he was beginning to proclaim that the 'Nieuwe Bouwen leans towards the finest Classical purity'.[23] Two years later he was to write that 'the reduction of Zakelijkheid to a simple formal dogma is based on a misunderstanding of our intentions'.[24] He went on to criticise the very concepts of the Nieuwe Zakelijkheid and the objectivity of International Bouwen, the former because it tended towards a belittling interpretation of architecture on the utilitarian and constructive plane, and the latter because it neglected national expressions, namely historical roots, traditions, customs and climate. Here we should not forget the presence of Grampré Molière at the Delft school, where, from 1925 onwards, he opposed Functionalist unilaterality, the formal restrictions of De Stijl and the expressionistic importance of the

Amsterdam school in favour of the *Heimatstijl* qualities of local tradition and the vernacular, even neo-medievalist flavour.

In 1935 Staal won the Prix de Rome, and in the commentary attached to his Le Corbusier-style design he speaks of 'monumentality' and 'ornament', indicating that Le Corbusier was perceived in terms of Classical rationality and Cubist lyricism. Staal is joined by Van Ravesteyn, who observed in 1936, 'Functionality and constructive, economic and social considerations are guidelines but certainly not the essence of architecture'. He summons artistic principles back to 'beauty', accusing his colleagues of the Dutch characteristics of over-simplicity and puritanism and therefore of lack of imagination in their adherence to Functionalist dogma. What gave rise to the debate was actually Van Ravesteyn's office building in Utrecht, in a sort of French-style 1930s neo-Baroque. Staal, who considered the work very important, asked, 'Are we forgetting that we must be architects and not economists or statesmen? What could be at stake more important to us than a perfect concept for a perfect kitchen?' And again, 'Banks, town halls and public buildings are not houses, gardens and kitchens, they are Architecture with a capital A, and factors intervene that must not be limited – monumentality and ornament'.[25]

Staal's summons to architecture was firm – today we would call it disciplinarian – and found its supporters. In 1938 Boeken wrote of El Lissitsky, 'The man of "Proun" – one of the artistic "isms" without the "ism" – said in 1924, "Proun is the interchange station from painting to architecture". Good Heavens, in 1938 the ism-lovers are still sitting in the waiting room. We architects have travelled on. We have learned from the demonstrations, the content and the clarity of many of those artistic isms. We have understood that we ought to change trains and we have gone away to build. We have grown out of the vague aestheticism of "modern architecture".'[26]

Arthur Staal's design for Huizen Town Hall is a clear evocation of eighteenth-century Classicism; the symmetrical edifice dominates the garden with the great Neptune fountain and a double flight of steps with balustrade giving access to the main floor. Covered by a dome with a lantern housing a clock, and flanked by two small, glassed *dependences*, Staal's design, with a certain provocative candour, is virtually a naive tribute to the Dutch tradition of Classicism in the style of Van Campen; Pliny rewritten by Calvin.

This was naturally the occasion to open discussions and split the De Otto group, even though Staal and Van Woerden, associated designers, remained isolated. But Staal replies, 'The question does not lie in this little town hall! . . . The considerations that have been debated during the two years of the competition for the Amsterdam Town Hall have led to the recognition that there will be monumental architecture and that it is as wrong to make all buildings monumental as to make them all falsely ordinary.' On the other hand, faced with the radical-isation of the debate between the two groups, those who, 'hard as nails, only want to build little rectangular boxes, and the exiled élite who have discovered the new architecture and can no longer collaborate with those retrogrades,'[27] adversaries like Lacroix ask themselves, 'When does a building become monumental? Is the design for Huizen monumental? What defines this monumental archi-

Willem-Marinus Dudok:
Hilversum Town Hall,
1928–1930.

tecture? The ageing attributes that have still so superficially penetrated our lives? So it is impossible, is it, for a modern architect to shape something we may call monumental without using this clutter of forms?"[28] The problem came up again with the competition for the Amsterdam Town Hall, where Formalism prevailed over any difference in language, which swung from Romanic evocation to quotation from Berlage, neo-Renaissance echoes or neo-Gothic revisitation. The theme was perhaps too demanding; a building can hardly be expected to represent the rich and powerful Amsterdam and complete a triptych with the historic Rijksmuseum and the Exchange.

The most notorious episode, which has provoked the condemnation of historians and the most heated criticism, concerns the conversion of one of the greatest masters of modern Dutch architecture, Jacopus Johannes Peter Oud. Considered one of the major masters of rationalism, always isolated because, unlike Le Corbusier, Gropius and Mies van der Rohe, he did not run a school, he did not argue, he remained alone in thoughtful contemplation of his work, he produced, principally in Rotterdam, some of the most famous and rarefied districts of modern architecture. He did not believe in working partnerships and, crossing swords with Gropius ('My colleague Walter Gropius – whose works I would call "choral" architecture – may detest the architecture of the prima donnas, but I doubt that a world conforming entirely to his architectonic canons would turn out to be very attractive.')[29], he asserted that the anonymous school of architecture was the expression of the sheep rather than the shepherd. Oud felt that the phenomenon of collaboration was due to 'diminished consideration of architecture's figurative value'.[30] One may ask for the

Sybold van Ravesteyn: main entrance to Blijdorps Zoo, 1940.

sake of argument, what if a 'Frank Lloyd Wright society' or a 'Mies van der Rohe society' existed? Has anyone ever heard of a 'Toscanini society' even though the merits of his orchestra should not be under-valued? 'Working in collaboration,' proclaimed Oud, 'indicates for me a loss of spiritual quality because its result lacks the clarity and purity of a synthesis.'[31]

The Shell building at The Hague, begun in 1938 (but finished in 1942), is considered the bone of contention. The building is a grand attempt at synthesis between certain elements of rationalist language, for example the great glassed-in spiral staircase on the head of the main factory body, or the insertion of curved factory units on a circular plan into the stem of the T, together with the strongly symmetrical layout which provoked the Beaux-Arts scandal, and an emphatic

Jacopus Johannes Peter Oud: Shell Building,
The Hague, 1938–42.

(*above*) The rear of the building. (*below*) The
refectory, and detailing of the façade.

monumentalism in the rhythmic repetition of the elements, concluding with the return of unashamedly decorative themes, which have a plastic and formal function. But this kind of counterpoint is not entrusted to the presence of statuary, being instead designed as an exercise within the architecture, tending to suggest a slight oriental echo, that exotic vein never far from the Dutch spirit; it also suggests geometry, whose efficiency at engendering post-war formalism was to prove no less marked than the cries of condemnation provoked by the work from the orthodox champions of modernism. Certainly it is hard to agree with everything about the Shell building, mainly because some formal details are extrinsic and dated. But outside the usual reservations it must be recognised that the force of synthesis achieved by Oud between Classicist balance and the modern language is courageous and altogether resolved in many aspects in a masterly way; actually it was this very attempt at synthesis that determined a certain drop in tension.

Before concluding it is worth summarising Oud's philosophy, even though the facts lie outside the timespan of this work. Oud gave a lecture at The Hague in 1951, on the occasion of the Congress of the International Association of Art Critics, which had its headquarters in the much discussed Shell building. This building had been condemned by *The Architectural Record*, who wrote, 'Here Oud goes on to embroider. The plan of this building is hardly distinguishable from more academic works, its shapes do not arise from specific building terms but seem drawn from a collection of architectonic notes. The insistent, isolated, and heavy decorative motifs seem to refer to pleasant reminiscences of rustic art rather than to a process of major perceptual acumen.'[32] Oud replied, denying that domestic architecture was itself the new architecture, but conceding that it could be its basis and drawing attention to the difference between architecture that serves a purpose within the sphere of daily life and that which fulfils a symbolic function. 'Architecture old and new,' proclaimed Oud, 'can and must stimulate an emotion, it must transfer the aesthetic vision from one man, the architect, to another, the observer.' Oud even quoted Spengler's *Decline of the West* to declare that architecture could still embrace art, that the architect must go back to being an artist, he must 'impregnate the building activity with his feeling, his spirit, a spirit of highly aesthetic order,' that architecture certainly involves rational principles, but 'the secret of architecture lies today as always in art. We must discover this truth in ourselves, that architecture is a spiritual problem.'[33] Nor did he spare the leading figures of contemporary architecture: Le Corbusier 'passed from architecture to the epic, to technique, to playing puzzle games on society'. The 'luminous and spacious factory houses of Neutra have architectonic pretensions but very little to do with architecture'. Gropius, so 'reasonable and honest, is too concerned with ethical, technical and social problems'. The only one who escapes is Frank Lloyd Wright: 'What an artist!' In fact the Shell building is an 'effort to rediscover architecture as the expression of the spirit. Consequently you will find in it elements that over the years have proved themselves good conductors of psychological feelings founded on universal understanding. They concern geometry, symmetry, harmony, proportion and even, here and there, hierarchy. In addition, matters concerning modules, ornamentation and so on have been dealt with. Different styles are based on the same aesthetic schemes, and experience has demonstrated that even adopting them it is possible to achieve infinite variety in external appearance, as happens with millions of human faces based on the same skeleton.'[34] The plan is not a dead academic figure, but has grown from a more functional aesthetic impulse, 'an impulse in which Functionalism expresses itself in delight'. Decoration was not born to hide the construction but is structually bound to it; it is not 'only an ornament to look at, but joyously gives shape to the necessities of life'.

It is this very serenity, not lacking in points of argument, but objective and gentlemanly, even though the cultural instruments and the method are a little old fashioned, that compelled respect even from opponents, such as Bruno Zevi of that incomparable journal *Metron*, and flung open the windows of Italian architecture to the world after a period of stuffy independence. And it is above all this hymn to joy, rather ironically chanted on the eve of the Second World War and the years that were to cost Holland so much suffering and laceration, that compelsl not only respect, but a more careful evaluation of Oud's position, quite apart from the schematic classi-fication of avant-garde or rearguard. It constituted an impossible attempt to mediate between two worlds.

THE MONUMENTAL ORDER IN SCANDINAVIA: RECURRING THEMES

In the principal European nations the 1930s style, very much a return to Classicism, represented a rallying of the spirits after the anxious period following the First World War, during which the avant-garde was dismembered and eclipsed; this can be summed up in the formula 'return to order'. But the situation in Scandinavia was completely different, even, in a sense, quite opposite; the effects of the war had not been felt there in the same way, and during the period following the 1920s resources were mainly concentrated in social reform. (Finland represents a separate case: after it had recovered its national identity its internal tensions erupted in civil war.) But Classicism, perhaps because of the Scandinavian frame of reference, was solidly institutionalised in architecture during the twenty years 1910–1930. It is no accident that an important exhibition[35] was devoted to this very theme in 1982, advancing the theory that Scandinavia was the cradle of the post-modern or, if this assertion may seem contentious, at least showing how a number of coincidences and anticipations of more recent experiments in contemporary architecture may be found in Scandinavian drawings, designs, and completed buildings dating from before 1930.

The origins of this quest for a Neoclassical serenity, for subtle evocations of the architecture of the Enlightenment, even for occasional explicit quotations from Ledoux and Boullée, as in Asplund's famous Stockholm Public Library, can perhaps be found in the Nordic spirit. One can perhaps detect a natural contrast between rationalism and rationality, between the epic inclemency of nature and acute longings for the stillness of buildings and the mark of human civilisation expressed so profoundly by the concept of Classicism. One can perhaps detect also the contrast between an architecture defined as romantic, partly subject to English and partly to German influence. There is finally the marriage between vernacular and Classical styles, which inspired such a master as Tessin, and is to be found in that early masterpiece by Erik-Gunnar Asplund, the Chapel of the Cemetery in the Wood of 1918–1920.

When the Stockholm Exhibition opened on 16 May 1930, it also opened Sweden's age of rationalism. Unlike the rest of Europe, Scandinavia had not known the disruption consequent upon the Great War and the exhaustion of the avant-garde. Whereas in Europe Classicism was a response to a longing for a return to order, in Scandinavia it took a particular form, the refinement of design and of the human interpretation of rationalism, which was eventually to influence the whole architectural world and constitute one of the key elements in the Modern Movement. It is necessary to point out that Asplund's first attempt in the Functionalist vein was not intended as a manifesto but expressed instead a mature awareness, a convergence of Constructivist elements, quotations from Le Corbusier, and echoes of Swedish grace,[36] and appears to be a product of that intellectual refinement which Asplund had, in fact, consistently displayed in his early Classicist works.

Concert Hall, Stockholm, 1928 (sculpture by
Carl Milles, 1936).

Erik-Gunnar Asplund (1855–1940): extension
of Town Hall building, Gothenburg, 1934–7
(view and detail).

Erik-Gunnar Asplund: three views of Stockholm
Cemetery Crematorium, 1935–40.

Erik-Gunnar Asplund: three views of Stockholm
Public Library, 1928–29.

Indeed, Nordic Classicism had never come to a total halt, since the preceding decade had already seen the realisation, following all the Classical rules, of Ivar Tengbom's Konserthus, the famous hall where the Nobel prizes are awarded, and Asplund's early experiments with the Gothenburg Town Hall extension, which took Tessin's Classicism and added a witty and refined series of variants ranging from an independent design of the Classical type to a functionalist complex with elements of a decorative nature (which unfortunately provided a model for straightforward imitation for all the refurbishments of historic centres, particularly in Italy, after the Second World War). And again, in the Stockholm Public Library of 1928, the echoes of Ledoux, La Villette and Boullée are quite obvious, but are redeemed by the refinement that Asplund managed to impart to every detail, while the specifically Swedish character lends an air of formal subtlety to all the elements, whether inventions or Classical quotations. In the famous Stockholm Cemetery Crematorium of 1935–40, which falls at the end of the timespan with which we are concerned, Asplund succeeded in combining the blood-curdling yet romantic howl of the wind in the virgin forest and over the great meadows, a rarefied Classicism with marble cross and open portico, and the aggressive functionality of the crematorium, where even the mouths of the furnaces are exactly shaped to admit a coffin. Thus he succeeds in giving to each part, each functional element, not only its own shape but also its own essential symbolic form, so that nature is nature, the cross is cross without a base or any other architecture but itself, the meadow is meadow, the wood is wood, and everything in the austere solemnity of the place exudes an impression of finality and proclaims indeed a final symbolic message.

We could also cite the Stockholm Maritime Museum by Ragnar Östberg, which in 1939 concluded the attempt at a balance between rationalism and Classicism – a Classicism which comes from afar – and has given rise to talk of 'Scandinavian Doricism'.[37] The position of Classicism within the Swedish architectural language should be more closely defined. Because if we speak of Classicism or, trying to be more precise, of Doricism, and make references to Boullée, Ledoux, Schinkel and Gilly, we do no more than record the evidence; but the matter becomes more complex if we investigate how those quotations are produced, or the links established with the general European situation, or the nature of the by no means simple utterances of that which could be called the 'genius of the people' at the heart of a generic Scandinavian or Nordic model.

Apart from the work of Asplund, it is worth considering also the early works of Cyrillus Johansson and the orthodoxy of Sigurd Lewerentz, which still permitted, in the manner of Sven Markelius, a modernistic note.

Denmark, in the same period, treated the same problems and the same architectural vocabulary with somewhat different inflections. Take Hack Kampmann, the old master of the new Carlsberg Glyptotek, who, shortly before his death in the 1920s, lent his influence to the design for the police headquarters; his great round courtyard with its Classical portico helped to create the town-planning vision of Steen Eiler Rasmussen.

Johan Sigfrid Sirén:
Parliament building,
Helsinki, 1937.

In Finland, political and social upheaval has never been allowed to stand in the way of a longing for that serenity and power expressed in the Parliament building constructed by Johan Sigfrid Sirén between 1924 and 1930, or characteristic of the early work of Alvar Aalto, who returned in his last period to planning Helsinki with so much dignity and environmental sensitivity.

In Norway, Neoclassicism was institutionalised from 1923 onwards within the Norwegian Academy of Architects in Oslo, culminating in the competition for Oslo University in 1926.

In fact specific examples and analogies in Scandinavia are interrelated in a complex and subtle way; they find their justification in a quiet meditative quality, a kind of distillation that reduces the formal legacy of the Classical world to the primitive, to a kind of metaphysics of the building process where the romantic and classical meet in the primeval world of the wooden hut, a reading of Laugier, in the mythology of the Doric order as the essence of building.

FRANCE

To conclude this panorama of national versions of the 1930s style we must examine France, because the notion of style was more integral in France, so much so that it can be considered the last historic style in French architecture. Style as a common language, a legacy of signs, recognisable, but at the same time a reference grid that did not exclude personal inflections and characterisations; style inasmuch as it summarised, symbolised and precisely corresponded to the haut-bourgeois scene, involving a Classicism that aimed above all at imparting a touch of class, and which held good even when this same bourgeoisie ran out of luck during the terrors and paralysis of the attacks following the establishment of the Popular Front, and the crisis preceding and centring on the defeat of 1940. But the achievement of the Popular Front was not socialist realism, it was the 1937 Exhibition and the Palais de Chaillot. The awakening, however, was brief; the Universal Exhibition opened on 1 May, and on 22 June Léon Blum resigned; many hopes were dashed, and this marked the start of France's most grisly period of decadence, anguish and instability.

The idea of a world in decline brought forward the figure of Valéry; Eupalinos concludes his design with a reassuring image, but, having lost its vitality, it became more and more the product of a 'style' – this time in the negative sense. Standard-bearers of the debate were Le Corbusier and Lurçat, two faces of modern functionalism, the former Protestant, Cartesian, dogmatic, his pen incisive, his designs typical of the mentality of a Swiss born in the country of clockmakers, and the other Mediterranean, Catholic, Communist, destined to disappear from the evolving panorama and to take refuge in his tapestry work. But Le Corbusier designed a penthouse in the Champs Elysées for Bestégui, a leading international society figure, with Louis XV commodes standing in full view between bright patios and large modern glass walls. *Eupalinos* nourished 'l'Esprit Nouveau'; white was in fashion, it assailed the sullen, sooty face of Haussmann's Paris, but maintained its precedents, proportions and lifestyle. Roux-Spitz, pupil of Tony Garnier, enjoyed unprecedented success; he set up a mega-studio, produced a series of buildings in which he constantly repeated his own trademark, conscious of the value of this repetition, this ease of identification which nevertheless makes it difficult for historians to place it – modern, classical, or classical-modern? Roux-Spitz did not theorise; when he wrote, he presented his work under a significant title, *Réalisations*: 'An architect's success, that is to say both commercial and social success, lies in the proportion he manages to maintain between trends and tradition. Between what he perceives as a fashion and the knowledge that comes from an academic education in the fine arts. He belongs to an architectural respectability balanced between conformism and poetry.'[38] His conviction of having hammered out a style with a certain value, a conviction strengthened by his success in the private urban sector, gave him the urge to build 'inserts' in the principal historic building complexes; this explains his involvement in the basements for the Bibliothèque Nationale.

But it is undoubtedly with the Palais de Chaillot, designed by Carlu, Azéma and Boileau, that the monumental order reaches its high

(*above*) Le Corbusier: terrace of the Bestégui
apartment on the Champs Elysées, 1930–31.
(*below*) Robert Mallet-Stevens: set for Marcel
L'Herbier's film *L'inhumaine*, 1923.

(*above*) Carlo Sarrabezolles: bronze group at
the Palais de Chaillot, 1937. (*below*) Robert
Delaunay: Maquette for the Railway pavilion at
the Paris International Exhibition, 1937.

Musée d'Art de la Ville de Paris, with sculptures by Drivier and Guénot and bas-reliefs by Janniot, 1937.

point, together with an attempt to strike a balance between modernism and Classicism, crystallised in the quotations from Paul Valéry that are inscribed there in golden letters. It should be explained that it was only Napoleon's Russian campaign and the stubborn resistance of a gardener (who had a little hut on the site and who appealed to the State Council which Napoleon had set up as a safeguard for the rights of the people), which prevented the emperor building the Palais de Chaillot for the king of Rome.[39] Here, as in the Trocadéro building, an inclination towards Classicism resulted in a work of impressive dimensions, monumental right down to its fountains. Today it forms part of the Paris cityscape; with the neighbouring Tokyo building, it splendidly represents the 1930s style and constitutes the last evidence of the supreme self-confidence of the Third Republic.

It was Perret who provided the means with his belief in an absolute where reason and sentiment merge and combine. But this has succeeded in creating an interpretative problem that contemporary critics and historians have largely failed to resolve. Looking at Perret's work in the 1930s, on the one hand, one can see the importance of his theoretical contribution (see Whittick, Rogers, Collins[40]); on the other hand, in the revision of his pioneering works – the house in the Rue Franklin and the Champs Elysées theatre – some have recognised a possible convergence between academicism and the Modern Move-

Roger-Henri Expert (1882–1955): French Embassy at Belgrade, 1934, with sculpture by Carlo Sarrabezolles.

ment (Banham[41]). Moreover, links have been identified between Perret's work and the architectonic culture of Neoclassical rationalism (Collins). In fact Perret's robust roots go back to Guadet and from him to Blondel and Laugier, while for Classicism, as it relates to France, he can turn to Choisy and his *Histoire de l'architecture* of 1899 based on rationalism.

Perret is the Eupalinos of reinforced concrete; as we have seen, he explored all the possibilities and offered them to both builders and imitators; he identified analytically the architectural language, and contributed more than anyone else to the monumental order. Mallet-Stevens, the Eupalinos of the great couturiers, paid his debt to Hoffmann with Cubist embroideries, while breaking new ground with set designs for Marcel Herbier's film *L'Inhumaine*, a kaleidoscope of lights and geometrical planes which was basically a secret confession of his ideal in architecture.

But in a sense the most French figure – if French implies primarily rationality and elegance – is that of Expert, whose unusual work takes in diplomatic buildings and great exhibitions – the Colonial Exhibition of 1931 in Paris and the 1939 Exhibition in New York – as well as large transatlantic liners such as the *Normandie*. Apart from a few schools and a few villas his work was carried out on a highly emblematic plane, where décor and architecture are synthesised in a vision that relates to the style of Louis XIV, purged of the Baroque but which still evokes it in terms of grandeur and elegance – one might almost say the elegance of its grandeur. The conventional terms – classical modern or modern classical – seem imprecise and inadequate to define it, while the term elegance, though more correct, seems somewhat generic. Expert taught alongside Gromort at the Ecole des Beaux-Arts for a certain period, and he brought·to 1930s architecture a sense of architecture's great institutionality, which lay at the heart of the French tradition and in particular the grand style of Louis XIV. Even Roux-Spitz, when he built his villa at Dinard, had shown signs of returning to the *maison de plaisance* style of the great architectural treatises. But Expert did not adhere to one code (although until 1925 one sees inevitable traces of Stoclet Hoffmann). In the restoration and reconstruction of Reims Town Hall, besides his great capacity for quoting styles from Louis XIII to Louis XIV, every aspect suggests a different possibility to him (even when Percier looms up behind Poiret underlying all is a Classical purity). In the 1930s Expert found himself expressing the ultimate in grandeur, his fairyland of water and lights for the Colonial Exhibition. Here he made no concessions to the exotic influence of Negro art; on the contrary, the themes suggested by that world were translated and virtually sublimated by a constant determination to stylise. In his French Embassy in Belgrade he expressed the identity of France in terms of pure Classicism; one rediscovers there again the elegance of figurative imagery and the refined décor of the *Normandie*.

Whereas Le Corbusier had advocated the sparse, rational language of naval engineering in his *Rappels* to architects, in the case of Expert architecture gave something back to transatlantic liners, and not only to the suites of the first-class saloons, which were the setting for sumptuous high life, a kind of daily pageant such as had not been seen since the days of Garnier and the Opéra; even where operational requirements were most directly applicable, Expert made the decks and promenades of the *Normandie* akin to the open spaces of a floating Versailles. Then, on the eve of the Second World War, he designed a complex interplay of volumes for the French pavilion at the New York World Fair, in which he delivered the final message of the power of *le grand goût*.

As between quotation and evocation, Expert's programme rested mainly on the latter; but where quotation means sticking to a model and entrusting oneself to the security of its intrinsic authority, evocation means filtering and distilling the 'traditional' matter and offering a concentrate capable of arousing the memory and producing analagous but not strictly imitative effects. The product of evocation is necessarily different, on a higher level of intellectual refinement, and runs greater risks. In the game of 'art for art's sake' the dividing line between the sublime and the banal is narrow; imagination walks a tightrope, now producing unprecedented feats of equilibrium, now plunging helplessly. It has been written of Expert that he 'responds to the demand for an architecture of elegance, mainly the concern of the fortunate classes who are experiencing both a heady freedom and the weight of tradition at the same time'.[42] Expert raised a monument to elegance, the enchantress who links the ephemeral with history, marries Erté with Mansart and architectural perspective with haute-couture models; he drew architecture out of its isolation – closely collaborating with a whole array of artists – and introduced a fairytale dimension which summed up the illusions of the twentieth century from the 1900 Exhibition onwards in a firework display that then yielded the night to the flares and tracers of war.

Tony Garnier (1869–1948): interior of the Town Hall at Boulogne-Billancourt, 1934.

INTERIORS: A MONUMENT TO THE ÉLITE

A year after the 1925 Paris Exhibition, furniture was for the first time included alongside the other arts in an aesthetic system that set out to construct great architecture; each art had its own role and all were of identical quality. Alain in his *Système des beaux-arts* suggested a great scheme for design that rejected empiricism, attempted to overcome Croce's mistrust of 'genres', and spread history out like a fabric, a web of situations and intentions set against the dry anthology of purely poetic creations.

'We can perceive the price of order,' wrote Alain. 'If we have not considered architecture that bears ornament, we cannot understand the rules of so-called decorative sculpture and painting. On the contrary, if we have well understood how a monument touches us, we are led quite easily to two principal rules. The first is that the ornament

145

Michel Roux-Spitz (1888–1957): annexe for
the Bibliothèque Nationale at Versailles,
1932–33.

Apartment in the Rue Litolff, Paris XVIème,
1939.

Michel Roux-Spitz: A villa at Dinard, 1938–9.
(*above*) Rotunda of the grand salon. (*below*)
Detail of the rotunda.

147

Roger-Henri Expert (1882–1955): Fountains for
the Paris Colonial Exhibition, 1931.

(*above*) Water theatre. (*below*) Totem fountain.

(*above*) The great signal. (*below*) Cactus fountain.

Interior of the liner *Normandie*.

(*above*) First-class dining room. (*below*) Tourist-class dining room.

(above) Bronze door to the dining room, by Raymond Subes. (below) Statue of La Normandie by Léon Baudry. Beyond, the smoking room and 'grand salon'.

(from top to bottom) Private dining room; lounge of the Honfleur suite, by Huet-Tchumy-Vermeil; drawing for crew quarters.

should be taken from the material itself, as though its purpose were to show off its texture and quality.'[43]

This pertinence of material and ornament leads to the rule that 'the ornament should never dissemble the requirements of the material, nor the work those of the mason'. And it follows that 'the finish, the grooving, the sharp angles are ornaments, for only the most durable stone preserves the finish and the edge ... Hard stones do not lend themselves to fragile reliefs, because the very hardness of the stone causes it to fracture under the action of the tool; low relief is therefore the rule for sculpted ornament. And it is certainly the reason why ornamental paintings and drawings should avoid even the appearance of fragile reliefs. Add to this the obligation to paint as close as possible to the material. These two strict conditions have deterred painters from copying things in all their detail, and have urged painting and drawing along arid paths, but also conducted them well beyond imagery. Speaking solely of ornament, it is patent that style here consists principally of simplified forms and flattened reliefs and is in fact governed by considerations of resistance and durability; in addition, time simplifies further, making errors of taste disappear, so that here progress comes of wear and ageing. No sooner does ornamental art overcome these difficulties, than it gets lost in confused forms and falls into the ridiculous trap of trying to rival the things themselves. "How pointless," said Pascal, "is painting which attracts admiration for resembling something if one does not admire the real thing!" . . . According to the second rule, ornament should never conceal the joins between stones; and here again time undertakes to efface any untruths the sculptor may allow himself. By the same reasoning the art of stained glass should never attempt to conceal the lead armature – in fact it cannot do so. These arts that cannot deceive are the true school of the sculptor and the painter, so is the art of decorating pottery, which has such limited means at its disposal. Furthermore the property of ornament is firstly to conform to the shape of the thing to be ornamented. We perceive here a remarkable analogy between ornamental arts and written language. Elegance in a phrase, always ugly, consists in trying to hide, so to speak, the joins between the stones, and twisting the words to describe the things; this is the sure sign of perishable work. For the words of common language and the liaisons of syntax are like hard stones and cement.'[44]

So here, in an age with as yet no suspicion of structuralism, Alain suggests a parallel between the language of words and the architectonic language of ornament. Let us look again at his essay on furniture. 'The artist should consider only when guiding his tool. The briefest study of fine furniture makes this sufficiently obvious, for it is perhaps in the art of furniture-making that style is best recognised.' Here we are at the opposite extreme to Le Corbusier's idea of standard furniture. And Alain goes on, alluding to the fashion for veneers fostered by Art Deco and practised well into the 1930s, 'The idea of joining different woods, or simply two pieces of the same wood but oriented differently, is a carpenter's idea; this is the way those solid blocks are made from which aeroplane propellers are cut. And ornament, as in parquets, is only a rule to be followed to make the small changes in the wood set

Jacques Emile Ruhlman (1879–1933): fluted
chiffonnier, 1928. Octagonal embossed key-
plate by Jeannot.

one another off. Thus ornament only marks out durable work. In the same way sculptures serve in the first place to render the solidity of the material used visible to the eyes. For, first, a fragile material does not lend itself to a sculptor's work, and, secondly, a poor wood or a thin, hollow piece of metal does not resist knocks and wear, and the shape testifies to this, or rather the shape and the material are testimony to each other. Thus the useful is manifest in ornament. For example, if a floor paved in rosewood lifts or deforms, the rosewood shows it; the same with marquetry. It is also quite plain at first glance that a chair with carved feet is not wobbly – there is no need to try it. Everyone must have noticed that beautiful armchairs are comfortable to sit in. But one cannot lie in them. Furniture of fine style (or simply "stylish" as the saying goes) is all for conversation and politeness; and it governs attitude and, through that, thoughts and feelings even more evidently than clothes do.'[45] His conclusion is that 'society must be supported by furniture, as women are by corsets'.[46]

This is an attempt to monumentalise furniture within a conceptual system, even though it basically represents a retrograde step compared with the approach to interior design that runs throughout all the great French treatises, where interior architecture, furniture, lighting, mirrors and so on are all totally integrated. Nevertheless it also corresponds to a taste for the single piece which is characteristic of the period in question, following the Art Nouveau concept of 'art dans tout' and just prior to the industrialisation of furniture-making. Emphasis was placed on the haut-bourgeois, élitist character of furniture which was much sought after and flaunted.

To find the origins of this development we must go back a few years to the 1925 Exhibition. Even Le Corbusier was affected by it; at that time his was a name for the élite to conjure with, even though he preached standardisation. 'From now on,' he said, 'it is easy to conclude that in everyday objects the artist will discover again élitist themes.'[47] The élitist spirit that emerged in Art Deco in the use of unusual materials and extremely refined forms Le Corbusier sought in the machine, which has its own cogent reality and a meaningful aesthetic. Taking his inspiration from the machine meant taking it from the principles of coherence. The Surrealists, however, in the name of creative incoherence, countered with useless machines, satirical machines that served no purpose. The machine aesthetic formed the pretext for a kind of intimacy between the machine and the imagination, which can never itself be mechanised. It is also possible to find in Le Corbusier at that time a vein of almost refined decadence: 'At the Guimet Museum there is a bronze Siva that I used to stroke surreptitiously with my fingers, simply to get the slight thrill provoked by an audacious word or gesture addressed to someone adored.'[48] We are nearer here to the Huysmans of A rebours than to the 'machine à habiter' (machine for living in). In his oriental journey, 'the disaster of Istanbul' is regarded as a 'grandiose spectacle'; l'Esprit Nouveau's dedication in its first issue is 'to reveal the unifying spirit that animates our society's various élites in their quests'.[49] It is in following this unifying spirit that we try to weave this difficult thread, but 'this new spirit that still only exists in a few people, the best in the arts and literature, must be helped to triumph resoundingly'.[50] Again in Vers

Apartment of Maurice Dufrène, Paris, c.1930.

Raymond Subes (ironwork), Paris International Exhibition, 1937: (*above*) doors in iron and bronze gilt in the About pavilion, Trocadéro palace. (*below*) Stainless steel entrance door to the Pavillon des Artistes décorateurs.

(*above*) Great door in bronze patiné of the Musée de la Ville de Paris. (*below*) Great door in wrought iron for the entrance to the Metal pavilion.

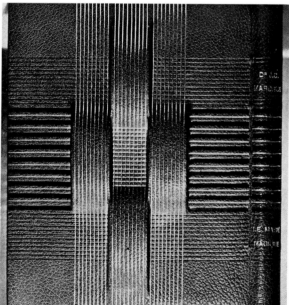

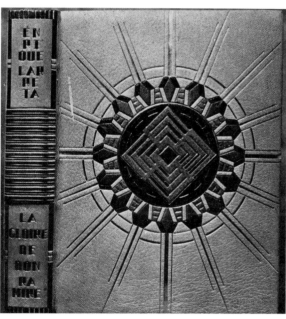

(*above*) Michel Kieffer: book cover in dark red morocco, with cabochon rubies and gold filets, 1938. (*below*) Artita Garcia: book cover in blue morocco with pale blue mosaic and decorations in gold, silver and pink, 1938. (*above right*) Paul Bonnet: book cover in salmon morocco, encrusted with lapis-lazuli motifs. (*below right*) Michel Kieffer: book cover in beige morocco with cabochons on gold plate, gold filets, 1938.

une architecture: 'The art of our time is in its right place when it is addressed to the élites. Art is not an affair of the common people, still less a de luxe prostitute; art is a nourishment uniquely necessary to the élites, who must group together if they want to become a guiding force; art is essentially part of the theme.'[51]

These are the tenets of the man who, more than any other, thought about the collective dimension of the city, so it only remains to seek the continuity and differences that exist between Art Deco and the language of the 1930s. Art Deco seems to be a selection and amalgamation of various elements that were available, cultural patterns and influences that rose to the surface ranging from the fashionable influence of primitive art, eclecticism and historicism, the Constructivist influence of De Stijl, and the geometric influence of Art Nouveau; so it can be said that Art Deco represents a distillation of all these ingredients. Art Deco set itself up as the antithesis of Art Nouveau's

157

(*above*) Auguste Perret: staircase in the Perret office, Rue Raynouard, Paris, 1930–33. (*below*) Raymond Subes: design for staircase ramp, Bély store, Paris, 1930.

(*above*) Bitherlin: staircase ramp in stainless steel, 1934. (*below*) Werner March: staircase for the Olympic Stadium, Berlin, 1934–36.

Raymond Subes:
wrought-iron staircase
for the Building Pavilion
at the Paris International
Exhibition, 1937.

naturalism, defining a geometrical world of elementary figures in various combinations that always appear logical, with a dynamism which carries over from Futurism. The visual juxtapositions produce violations, antitheses, transgressions; where parallel figures are employed improbable 'exits' are offered; the image leaves the flat plane, suggests three-dimensional spatiality, goes back; the game of logic is shattered, the rules of rhythm and the definition of alternations become obscure. The rendering is contradictory, that is it admits the simultaneous presence of verticals and diagonals, circles and coronets suggesting the movement of a clock mechanism, cogwheels that transmit conflicting rotations, complicated gears. When the same symmetry involves more than one axis, there is no longer an element of visual balance, such as a calm reversal of the image – serene specularity, but a counterpoising of forces all the more disquieting in that they are balanced, a picture of an equilibrium so unstable that it inevitably resolves itself into a kaleidoscope of splinters. In addition, violent colour associations are made to play a key role in this disturbing geometry.

By reworking reality in a satirical way, almost like an animated cartoon, and deliberately ignoring its fundamental principle of continuity, by using undulating curves, shading, aerial perspective, the language of Art Deco lies quite outside the line of descent from the Impressionists and feeds on the same elements used in the experiments of the figurative avant-garde. Unlike Art Nouveau, the formula is free of any social element, satirical, messianic or missionary. The élitist position – high quality, a rare piece, precious material, high cost

Jewellery by Jean Desprès: (*top to bottom*) Cup in silver, hammered and burnished, c.1937. Candlesticks in silver, hammered and burnished, c.1937. Set in hammered pewter and ebony, 1930–31.

(*top to bottom*) Ring in silver, 1937. Ring in silver and silver-gilt, c.1937. Ring in silver, silver-gilt and blue enamel, c.1935.

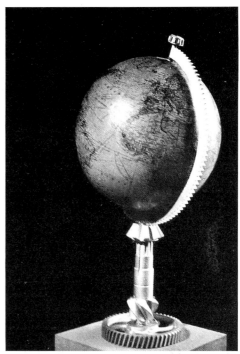

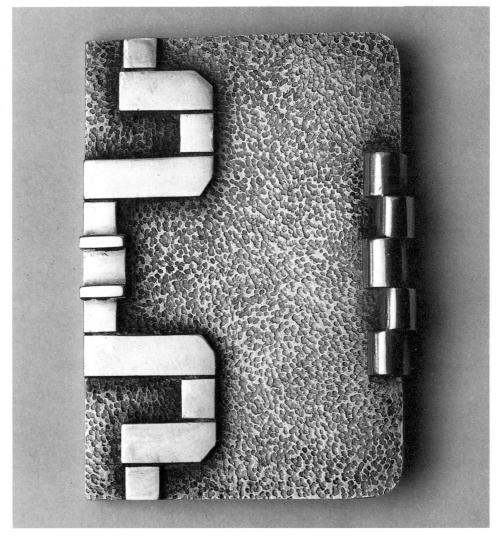

Jean Desprès: (*above*) Brooch in silver, silver-gilt and malachite, c.1937. (*below*) Vase with five horizontal sides, burnished pewter, 1937.

(*top left*) Clock made of automobile parts for Mr Henry Ford, c.1938. (*top right*) Illuminated globe made of automobile parts for Mr Henry Ford, c.1938. (*below*) Villebrequin brooch in silver, c.1930.

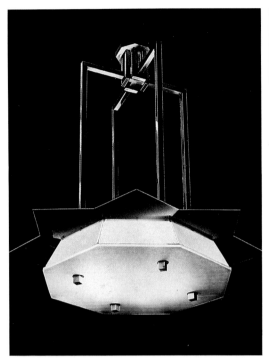

Photographs of light fittings in the National
Furniture Collection, Paris, c.1930.

Maurice Dufrène: lighting arrangement in the
Challes-les-Eaux casino, c.1930.

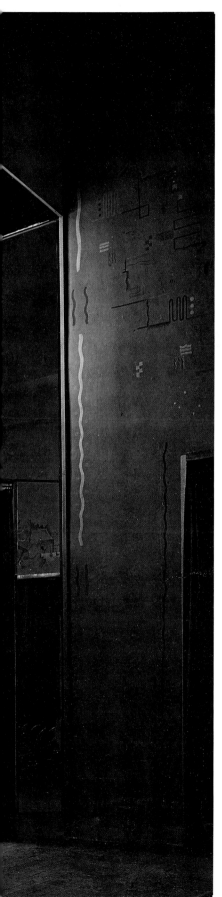

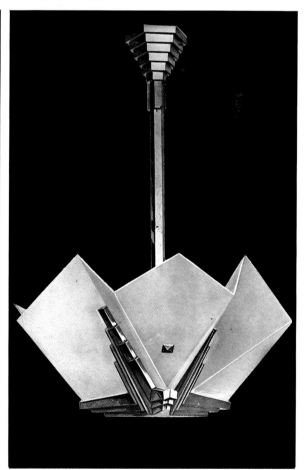

(above and bottom right) Photographs of light fittings in the National Furniture Collection, Paris, c.1930. (bottom left) Albert Simonet: 'Weeping Willow' light fitting in bronze and moulded glass, 1930.

and so on – tends if anything to appropriate incomprehensibility and rites of initiation (principles drawn from the avant-garde) and to translate them confidently into something commonplace. What was taking place in the realm of Art Deco may be described as the consummation of the avant-garde.

However, in the 1930s all this decorative apparatus and figurative abstraction was abandoned, and the needle of the compass swung round to one essential element: material. The relationship of material to shape as determined by refined execution, sometimes pushed almost beyond the intrinsic possibilities of the material, constituted another notion of rarity. The relationship between form and geometry grew clearer, became essential and concise, and – still in the spirit of the return to order – permitted the insertion of genuinely figurative elements into open spaces and between smooth and costly surfaces. This was a counterpart to Neoclassicism and involved among other things the introduction of sculpture into architectural settings: for example, the sculptures of Lipchitz in Le Corbusier's Cité universitaire.

The language of the 1930s began to resemble a research laboratory working with traditional techniques but on the lookout for novel materials. Research progressed along three lines, corresponding to the three leading figures in France: Jacques-Emile Ruhlmann with his exhaustive eclecticism, Chareau with his modernist openness, and Jean-Michel Frank with his geometric handling of material. Within Art Deco it was Ruhlmann who appeared as a purifier of line, proportion and material; his line is always tense, the curves never full, and the tension never violent but deriving from vertical elongation; the ivory motif on the foot which continues round the edges right up the piece of furniture, outlining it and giving it character, sometimes works in counterpoint with the full form of the piece. He always suggests a clear and rational play of structures, tending to give to individual elements a precise role, but at the same time attempting to express complete unity and perfect fusion of the various components. He emphasises this 'monolithic' quality by using monochrome material from which the adjuncts outlined in ivory or the simple contrast of woodgrain scarcely detracts. It is a language, in fact, which combines with a controlled and refined use of design the expressivity of the material, so that the material itself almost becomes linear. With the arrival of the 1930s, Ruhlmann seems to have become aware of the needs of the world in its current crisis, and he moved towards greater simplicity and fullness, renouncing his former slenderness and grace. But the simplicity did not extend to his budget; in 1932, to his 'Rendez-vous des pêcheurs de truites', the most important stand at the Salon des artistes décorateurs, he allotted 400,000 francs. He died shortly afterwards, in 1933. He had been the forerunner and leading figure of what Francis Jourdain termed 'démeubler'.

The monumental order had been anticipated in the furnishings of the Neoclassical Galerie des Glaces at Versailles in 1927, and the fitting out of the liner Île-de-France in the same year, where the Pombi Gallery noticed a neo-Doric quotation unusually associated with the wavy-edged parquet and the carpet: a bold combination of freedom and severity.

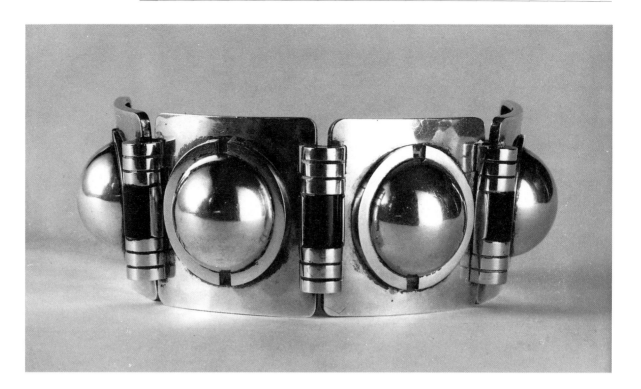

Jean Desprès: bracelet
in silver, silver-gilt and
onyx, 1930.

THE COLONIAL EXHIBITION OF 1931 AND COLONIAL ARCHITECTURE

The 1931 Colonial exhibition in Paris embodied the values of progress and rationalism – 'to colonise is to build' – and opened in an atmosphere that exemplified peace. Marshal Lyautey, organiser of the exhibition, who had learnt his lesson in 1915 at Casablanca, declared: we want 'to add to human gentleness the wild hearts of the savannah and the desert'.

The exhibition, erected as a temple to the glory of colonial politics, displayed its magic, its palaces and huts, its minarets and cupolas, on the banks of Lake Daumesnil. Appealing to the public's curiosity for the world outside Europe and with the slogan 'Around the world in one day' the 1931 exhibition presented itself as what would now be termed a Disneyland of indigenous cultures. Colonial architecture which attempts to show the value and the progress of Western civilisation in fact concedes very little to indigenous culture and there only remain some decorative motifs, such as the bas-reliefs of the sculptor Janniot for the Musée des colonies which symbolise 'the colonial art of inspiration'.

Whereas André Citroên reproduces his expeditions in the Sahara Desert and in China, Hagenbeck imports from Hamburg the African faun which has remained ever since in the Bois de Vincennes.

Conceived as a 'Great Event', following in the footsteps of the Palais des Illusions of the 1900 exhibition, the Colonial exhibition remains in people's memories for its prodigies of light and fountains. On the other hand, the language of the 1930s establishes itself overseas as a unifying force and represents the last moments of colonialism. Thus, Lutyens' New Delhi coincides with the crisis in British rule brought about by Gandhi. And, when Atatürk's Turkey turns towards Europe, it is to deny its own popular traditions and learning and identify with the Nazi Classicism of Holzmeister.

Albert Laprade and Léon Jaussely: preparatory drawing of the façade of the Musée des colonies, Paris, 1931.

Colonial Exhibition, Paris, 1931. (*above*)
Entrance. (*below*) Brasini: Italian pavilion.

(*above*) K. Alabian and S. Sofarian: Armenian pavilion at the Agricultural Economy Exhibition in Moscow, 1938. (*below*) House of Agriculture in Oran, Algeria, mid-1930s.

(*above*) Clemens Holzmeister: design for King Faisal's palace in Baghdad, 1932. (*below*) Pavilion of the Suez Company at the Colonial Exhibition, 1931.

(*top to bottom*) Maison du colon in Mascara, Algeria, 1938 — Edouard and Jean Niermans: design for the Town Hall in Algiers. Artist's impression of the main façade, 1934 — State Bank in Casablanca, Morocco, 1940.

THE 1937 EXHIBITION

The Paris Exhibition of 1937, coinciding with the brief period of the Popular Front, opened its doors amid a climate of social and political uncertainty. Fifty nations were represented. Léon Blum, Président du Conseil, was pensive: 'this encounter is the last hope for peace in Europe'.

The exhibition displayed the traditional array of national pavilions. The image presented by a democratic Europe was of a Classicism gliding towards decadence, with rhetoric, common to all nations, surmounting their differences. The unifying element *par excellence* was rhythm, indeed repetition – an obsessional cadence which saw Classical harmony being transformed into the sinister goose-step. Classicism, the symbol of equilibrium, thus becomes a messenger of terror. The image of this manifestation remains for the whole world the two imposing towers of the German and Russian pavilions, confronting each other face to face, each crowned with its own sculptural symbols.

The large frescoes by Robert Delaunay in the Rail and Air pavilion mark the triumph of aesthetics, the happy marriage of abstract art and monumental architecture. Raoul Dufy, on the other hand, worships the goddess Electricity in the Palais des Lumières in a dazzling spread covering a surface of 600 square metres. The pavilion devoted to the cinema, photography and the phonograph coincided with the first television transmission from the Eiffel Tower, and the triumph, in the theatre, of Louis Jouvet, named 'Man of '37'.

The exhibition was a failure due to poor attendances and the considerable costs involved. Inaugurated by President Lebrun in a large hall of the Trocadéro the exhibition was intended to be a feast of light, a symbol of equilibrium and Classical harmony – it marked, in reality, the last faltering steps of a Europe which was about to be engulfed in chaos.

Panorama of the Paris International Exhibition of 1937.

220. - PAVILLON DE L'ANGLETERRE

EXPOSITION INTERNATIONALE
PARIS 1937

104 - PAVILLON DE LA BELGIQUE

181. - VUE D'ENSEMBLE, PRISE DU PAVILLON DE L'ANGLETERRE

85. - PAVILLON DE L'ITALIE

233. - PAVILLON DE LA RADIO

234 - PAVILLON DE L'AERONAUTIQUE

Series of postcards published for the occasion, showing the pavilions of each participating country.

171

(*above*) Austrian pavilion. (*below*) Hall in the
Italian pavilion.

Photograph by Gaston Paris for the Paris
International Exhibition, 1937.

Grand ceremonial room in the Musée des
colonies, Paris, 1931. Furniture and parquet by
Prinz, frescoes by M. and Mme Lemaitre.

MATERIALS

A wider choice of materials had already been brought to interior decoration by Art Deco. Unusual ones such as galuchat[1] had become fashionable and a vast range of exotic woods had been tried out, while the use of metal had been extended and sophisticated. The art of marquetry, after a period of mimicking Art Nouveau, had rediscovered eighteenth-century geometric abstraction, and introduced new forms which were either powerful or simple, in line with the two directions taken by experiments in the decorative arts at that time.

The move towards a 1930s style came gradually, in the form of geometrical simplification or even the repudiation of decoration altogether in favour of mass, volume and stereometric clarity. This austerity led to material being evaluated in two ways, one concerned with its own intrinsic quality, the other with the way in which it lent itself to workmanship: both were inextricably linked. Difficulties of workmanship were to some extent overcome by the semi-industrial-isation and part-mechanisation of the work, offering the pre-production of slices of wood, large sheets of veneer, or blocks of marble sawn into thin slabs by new jigs.

The aim of this work was to place value on simplicity, in the face of one of the most widespread prejudices, in fact one of the man in the street's instinctive criteria for appreciation, that anything intricately worked is artistic, and the more richly and finely worked it is, the greater is its beauty. But to bring about a simplification, to make 'less' accept-able rather than 'more', the 'less' had to be quite exceptional, élitist if not unique. And as the Mannerists had found, this exceptional quality could not be entrusted to anything but the 'prodigy' of the material. But whereas the Mannerists had re-designed and re-absorbed their material – the natural element, that is – into an artistic object, such as a shell made into the body of a vase with bronze accessories, now the material was exclusively entrusted with the ennoblement of simplicity by a direct and close relationship between material and geometry. A pure surface – without joins, markings or the least irregularity, as wide a plane as possible – presents in itself some difficulty in workmanship; it needs delicacy and adroit assembly. There is also a risk of its durability being affected by variations in temperature from outdoor sun or indoor heating, and this in turn can involve special technology and lead to higher costs. Simplicity is expensive, and this very fact makes it élitist. The curve, the joining of two planes with a curved corner, the cylinder, the sphere and the half-sphere are all important dynamic elements arising from elementary solid geometry, which now became

Details of furniture by Jacques-Émile
Ruhlmann: (*above*) Facetted spindle-leg in
burr-amboyna, c.1928. (*below*) Foot-joint of
display cabinet in American burr-walnut, 1925.

Jean-Michel Frank: Two details of a cupboard
in straw-marquetry, 1935.

Clément Mere: detail of a cupboard in ivory
and Macassar ebony, 1928.

Jacques-Emile
Ruhlmann: front of an
amboyna chiffonier,
c.1922–23.

the basic language of architecture and interior design. The curve heightens the value of the material, producing incomparably interesting effects under various lights, but it is difficult to construct a curve in any material with a grain, in fact in any material that is not isotropic or synthetic. Hence the preciousness, technological value and finesse of anything curved. Simply veneering a wooden surface, even of modest size, is difficult, because wood veneer has a grain and this makes the material behave differently in different places; so a double curve (in two spatial planes) presents an even greater problem.

The quest for intrinsic monumentality that pervaded furniture design in the 1930s was devoted to the resolution of these elementary problems. Monumentality was coherent both in furniture and in architecture, and consisted of heightening values and accentuating

Clément Mere: detail of a cupboard in ivory and Macassar ebony, 1928.

the rapport between mass and material in order to draw out the maximum expressive quality. This possibility was enhanced by a series of cunning techniques that demanded considerable ingenuity on the part of designers. Great efforts were made to disguise joins, to hide hinges, to make marble or stone facings pass for solid blocks, to invent complex systems of balance, to devise angle pins, in short to eliminate as far as possible anything that gave the impression of structurally connected elements, in favour of a compact, homogeneous mass. The monolith is a kind of monument, elemental, instinctive, and the obelisk is its immediate interpretation, triumphant in technique, respectful of the prodigy of nature since ancient times. Where the compactness of the 'monomaterial' was insufficient they had recourse to the rapport between a geometric network and the material itself; Frank, as already mentioned, was a master of this type of mosaic. I have deliberately chosen the word 'network' because a closed geometrical design with a beginning and an end was not called for, but simply a fabric, a reference grid, or a constant rhythmic system devised on purpose to counteract by its own discipline and consistency any variation in the material. The relationship between artifice and nature was reduced to the essential dialectic between geometric formality and informality. From this dialectic derived the maximum appreciation of that variation, that is to say the specific and intrinsic qualities of the material.

As for the range of materials, one trend involved the readoption of those traditional materials which can render acceptable something potentially disruptive such as modern architecture in a historic city, or modern furniture clashing with 'period' style. But to deal with these

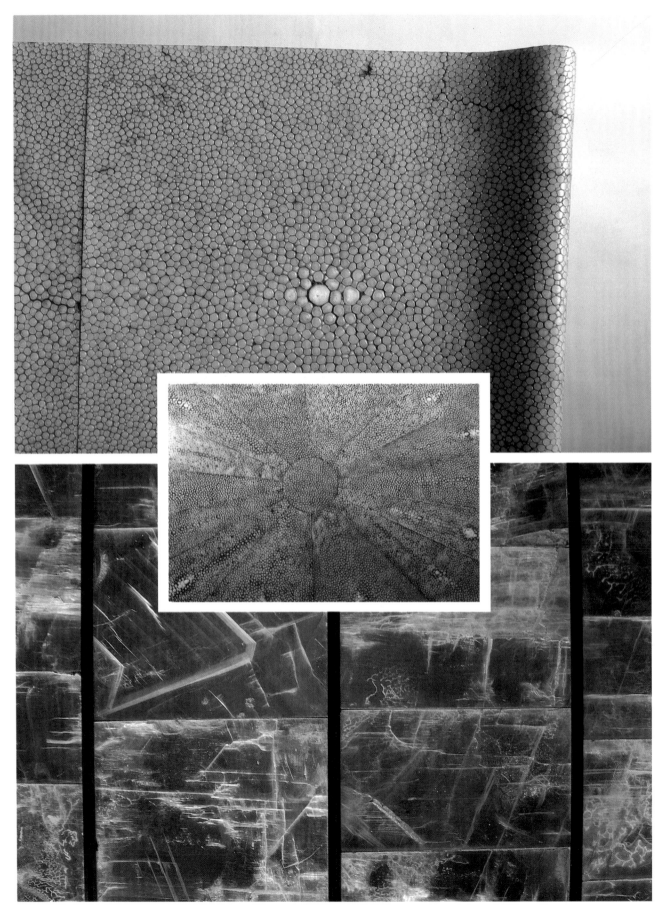

Jean-Michel Frank (1895–1965): (*above*) detail of a footstool in galuchat (sharkskin) with pagoda-shaped ends, c.1929. (*below*) Detail of a small cupboard with plaques of gypsum set in the bronze uprights, c.1929.

(*inset*) Detail of a piece of furniture upholstered with a radiating patchwork of galuchat, 1927.

materials, as I said, new techniques involving machines were offering new possibilities. As in the nineteenth century, progress continued in the direction of achieving today what was impossible yesterday.

Another trend was the search already started by Art Nouveau for a new spectrum of natural materials. The colonies offered a storehouse of materials that satisfied the craving for the exotic or simply for novelty, without further reference to the primitive cultures themselves. Paradoxically, while contemporary primitive art, primarily African, taught the expressive possibilities of unsophisticated material, the countries where that art originated offered Europe a precious commodity – for they were potential mines of the imagination, a source of the marvels of an unexplored nature.

This then was the new frontier of the decorative arts in the 1930s. From the turn of the century until that time, designers had been pushing this frontier ever further afield, and when this movement was exhausted, they had to look for new territory to conquer within the Western world; they found it with the machine. Not only had the machine offered Futurism its formal and dynamic pretexts, and not only had machine aesthetics given modern architectural forms the support of a functional logic, but the material itself directly relished the intervention of the machine, for its surfaces, relished the turning and milling achieved by the machine's mechanisms, the refined technology presiding over its construction. The world of industry, technology and applied sciences offered yet another territory to invade, and that was man-made materials. For diverse reasons a whole series of man-made materials were tried out during the 1930s, beginning with the introduction of plastics. We can think of this as the infancy of man-made materials, and like a child they seem at first to have imitated their parent, nature. Rubber imitated marble, celluloid imitated glass, rayon imitated silk, and there was artificial cork, ivorite or mock ivory, mock tortoise-shell and several more. It seems that this ability to imitate was in itself a virtue, offering what customers expected, while providing the wherewithal to avoid the working drawbacks and limitations of natural materials by the adoption of more manageable ones. In other words, appearances were preserved while materials and techniques changed, making production more economical and more up-to-date, and escaping the limitations imposed by the unavailability of rare materials. These new materials were entirely acceptable because they looked familiar, they fitted into a traditional aesthetic system, a traditional scale of values.

Ironically, the production of new materials for decoration led to a colossal fabrication of forgeries. Only through true machine aesthetics were new materials able to assume their own identity without recourse to imitation or counterfeit – as the radio, for example, developed from a piece of furniture to a piece of equipment. But even this was to become an élitist process, as the concept of 'decoration' was transformed into 'design' during and after the Second World War.

Another innovation was the artificial modification of natural materials, mainly wood. It was Hoffmann who introduced the technique of treating wood with a white or greenish plaster which penetrated the softer and more porous fibres and brought out the grain and cut. It had its origins in the popular art tradition of the rural community into which Hoffmann was born, and which constituted a common heritage that survived the break-up of the Habsburg empire into independent nations, an outstanding example of the tradition loosely known as 'rustic'. It is true that this treatment of wood enhances its characteristics, especially for oak, chestnut and all woods of porous grain, but at the same time it falls halfway between the liberation of the material's natural eloquence and the quest for novelty in the realm of artificial materials.

Finally we come to glass. The epic development of glass has its origins in the nineteenth century, but it was in the 1930s that industrial experiment opened up a startling new range of products. We are not thinking solely of the great sheets of transparent crystal or plate glass, nor of the numerous glazed façades that have become a cliché of modern architectural language, but rather of what was accomplished in the decorative arts. Here new products were developed, such as thermolux glass, two layers of glass enclosing a layer of glass fibre, with both translucence and insulating properties; prismatic glass with an opalescent quality that made it ideal for chandeliers; glass bricks of very thick crystal, suitable even for building purposes; finally a whole rainbow of mirrors, pink, blue, and steely, and that sort of mirror veneer made of tiny rectangles of mirror on an adhesive background, used to line furniture and capable of adhering even to quite steep curves thanks to its fragmentary nature.

Glass cement offered the possibilities of transparent fittings to replace the old reinforced glass of nineteenth-century skylights; it was useful too for walls and other vertical structures. In his Maison de verre, Chareau attempted to create an integral poetry of glass that would be a high point of modern architecture, but in the event he did not achieve a truly architectonic result comparable with Le Corbusier's Villa Savoye. It fell halfway between the programmatic and the experimental, like an exhibition pavilion made permanent. In actual exhibitions experiments were frequent, inspired by the novelty of the glass industry.

It was principally in connection with the decorative arts, as has been observed, that the new materials were exploited by the middle classes and indeed the general public. Early experiments were carried out on tempered glass, firstly for cars, then for buildings and furniture. In general, all these possibilities involved moving away from the idea that glass had to be a covering, a surface needing a support; innovations were now concerned with the independent structuring of glass, intent on making it as far as possible independent of metal or wooden supports, and aiming to achieve the maximum in terms of transparency.

This amounted in practice to monumentalising the material, attempting to extract to the utmost all its constructional and expressive potential; it enabled modern architecture and interior design to further the Gothic and Baroque quest for lightness, to research materials in an attempt to break free from static solidity, to escape from ponderous shapes to forms that fly.

There was a whole atmosphere of experiment abroad, involving architects and interior designers, among whom were personalities still little known, such as Pietro Chiesa of Milan, who was behind many

(*above*) Daum: vase, c.1930. (*bottom left*)
Marinot: large flask in colourless blown glass,
1930. (*bottom right*) Daum: vase in yellow
blown and cut glass, c.1930.

products and many novelties including decorative objects. The experimental revitalisation of the 1930s was also responsible for research in the field of coloured glass, which not only produced new materials such as pink crystal, smoked crystal and tinted mirrors, but led to a revival of the whole art of glasswork, from glass fired by traditional techniques to the extraordinary variety of blown glass of the Murano type. There were moves to develop its employment from single objects to a more general usage, creating evenly lit ceilings or great cascading chandeliers, and even trying out a series of opalescent effects with gold-impregnated glass, mainly the work of Venini and Barovieroso. Surpassing traditional methods, blown glass offered expanding possibilities for intensive and widespread use.

A. Coulon: Saint-Gobin table, 1937.

MATERIALS

Each age leaves a record of its ambitions, conflicts and dreams through the objects it hands on to posterity, the materials it chooses or invents, and the new forms it evolves.

The originality of creators of objects during the inter-war years lay in their massive use of rare and exotic materials that evoked distant lands. They produced objects in limited editions, aiming at an élite clientèle while also contributing to the setting of fashion.

Of particular significance is the work of the interior decorator Ruhlmann, who rehabilitated the idea of luxury and advocated furniture of great quality, employing highly-qualified staff to 'impose modern furniture on antique', as he said, adding, 'The beauty of pure, rational form interpreted in fine materials is persuasive'. Doubtless influenced by Cubism, interior decorators broke away from Art Nouveau with its complex interlacing ornament, its curvilinear forms and its naturalistic extremes. They preferred symmetry, simple forms, and costly material and decoration. Guided by the demands of comfort and an undeniable originality, they reintroduced furniture that evoked a somewhat obsolete way of life, such as the settee, the chiffonier and the small writing-table.

The first artificial materials, like imitation tortoiseshell, marble and glass, saw the light of day throughout the range of manufactured objects from jewellery to furniture. It seemed possible to reproduce the entire natural world. Both these imitation materials and plastics, fashioned and interpreted according to the laws of pure geometry, were the first steps on the road to mass production.

(*top to bottom*) Jean Goulden: Copper and enamel box, c.1930. Anonymous decorative lacquer panel, c.1930. Raoul Dufy: Earthenware vase, 1938.

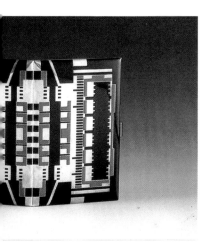

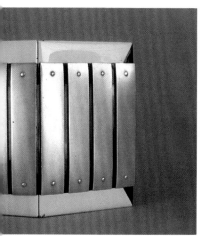

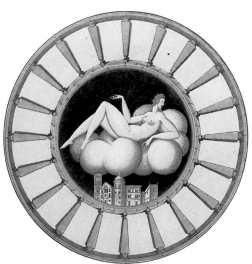

(*top to bottom*) Raymond Templier: silver and lacquer cigarette case, 1930. Raymond Templier: silver, aluminium and lacquer cigarette case, 1929. Raoul Dufy: ceramic vase, 1930.

Three works by Gio Ponti: (*above*) large 'Prospettica' earthenware vase. (*below*) Two earthenware plates in the 'My Women' series: 'Agata' (*left*) and 'Donatella' (*right*).

187

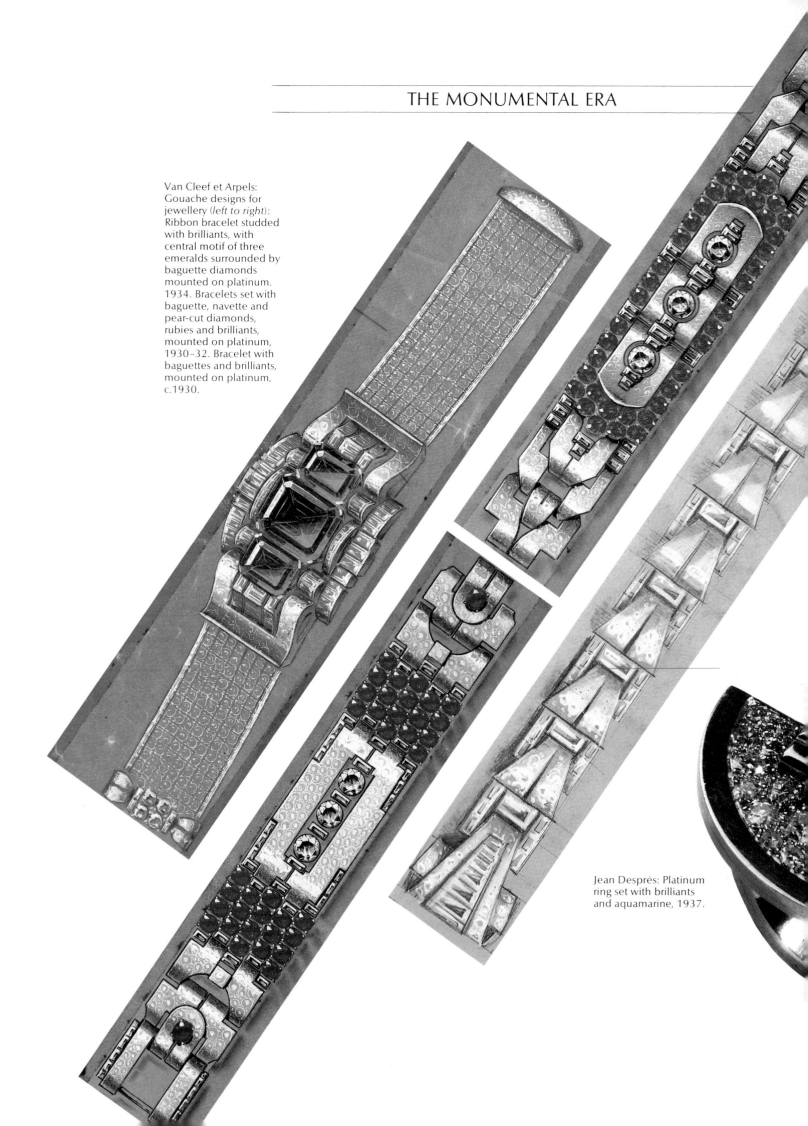

Van Cleef et Arpels: Gouache designs for jewellery (*left to right*): Ribbon bracelet studded with brilliants, with central motif of three emeralds surrounded by baguette diamonds mounted on platinum. 1934. Bracelets set with baguette, navette and pear-cut diamonds, rubies and brilliants, mounted on platinum, 1930–32. Bracelet with baguettes and brilliants, mounted on platinum, c.1930.

Jean Desprès: Platinum ring set with brilliants and aquamarine, 1937.

Van Cleef et Arpels: Gouache designs for jewellery: (*above*) Two serpent bracelets with four osmiore bands. The round central motif is decorated with a baguette diamond and brilliants mounted on platinum, 1936. (*below right*) Ribbon 'hexagon' bracelet, decorated with a buckle of round-cut diamonds, mounted on platinum, 1936. (*below left*) Ribbon 'ludo' bracelet, decorated with a central motif in baguette and trapeze-cut diamonds and brilliants mounted on platinum, 1936.

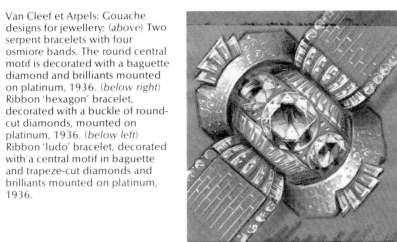

Gouache design for a choker necklace consisting of two adaptable or removable clips of baguette diamonds and brilliants on a serpent collar of osmiore, 1936.

Benedictus: Two studies for fabric prints from
the 'Relais' series, 1930.

René Braem: Imaginative drawing, 1933.

CONCLUSION: PERSPECTIVES

The success of the 1930s style is unusual in that it resides not in its historical authority, nor in the table of values it expresses, but in the inspiration it has given to present trends. Modern architecture, above all the post-modern, has rediscovered the values of Classicism, the institutional authority of architecture, aesthetic will-power. This is why modern examples of Classicism look to the past. Current events become history, and history is the teacher of life; the signpost of the guiding values that derive from the past is inverted, and the present brings the past into the limelight and sets it up if not as a model, then at least as a working theory; it is endorsed, made acceptable.

The 1930s form a bridge to carry the incarnation of Classicism into the history of modern architecture, a constant factor that nevertheless always varies with the variety of approaches to and the changing significance of whatever is interpreted as Classicism. The most common misconception is to consider it as something fixed and established, in short the concept of Classicism is too 'Neoclassic'. In actual fact the Classical code from the Renaissance onwards – and even earlier, as it traversed the Medieval and Gothic periods – underwent continual variations, or rather 'variants'. One variant of Classicism was the Utopian, visionary approach of the architects of the Enlightenment and the Revolution, another was the epic Napoleonic approach, which was the source of the Empire style. Neoclassical Classicism embodies both the values of universality and the national inflections corresponding to particular cultures, both the Academies and the leading interpreters of the popular spirit, in an even more emphatic way than does 1930s Classicism.

Classicism was a unifying force in the mosaic of the Italian states before Unification, in the German states before Bismarck, in the countries that comprised eastern Europe, in the relationship between Scotland and England, but its expression in each was subtly differentiated. The idea of Classicism ran through not only the rational model of Napoleonic Europe, but also through the Romantic movement, the fascination of ruins, confident and positive eclecticism, as well as the dream imagery of Symbolism. The idea of architectonic Classicism pervaded the final moments of the political order in central Europe that was to be toppled by the First World War, the Kaiser's imperialism, and the Secessionist ideal of 'Vienna-Byzantium'; it also accompanied the founding of the historic avant-gardes, and can be traced within the Modern Movement, in Le Corbusier and his more Utopian work, and in the geometric inflections of Art Deco.

Umberto Cuzzi: Design for the Via Roma in
Turin, 1933.

Alfred Chambon:
design for motorway
intersection, Brussels,
1938.

The line that had been advanced against by the masters of the Modern Movement from Oud to Gropius and Mies van der Rohe, and which had been considered to be in a state of capitulation and senility, in the end proved victorious. Louis Kahn, Philip Johnson, I.M. Pei, Edward Stone, Josef Kleihues, O.M. Ungers, Aldo Rossi, Franco Purini and Georgio Grassi, Ricardo Bofil and José Ignazio Linazasoro, Peter Eisenman and Rob and Leon Krier, each with a different accent – much more than the flippant quotations of the post-modern – delineated the prospects of a future for Classicism, almost indeed a classical Futurism, which, regardless of the critical fortunes attaching to particular personalities, the validity of their works and their possibilities of realisation, indicated a common determination to redeem architecture as such, and a need for 'aesthetics', a need for the 'monument'.

The critical panorama has changed. John Summerson's book *The Classical Language of Architecture*,[1] originally produced by the BBC in association with a television series, dealt with the concept of Classicism as a constant factor throughout the entire history of architecture, but his thesis was rejected by the anti-classicists. The entire 1930s style was expunged from the history of architecture, being portrayed simply as the results of academicism, of Beaux-Arts conservatism or as the art of dictatorships. Nevertheless, the tide of history has brought about the rediscovery of the Classical, this time even with naif accents, with ingenuities to compensate for the loss of visual and graphic culture, of nomenclature, language, morphology and professional competence, all worn out by years of rejection and facile condemnation as academic rubbish.

The 'return to order' signifies the need for a fundamental constant, that of the monument. The old litany mentions five orders: Doric, Ionic, Corinthian, Composite and Tuscan, keeping quiet about the various attempts to found national orders, principally French. The 'order' of the orders, the least common denominator which unites and distinguishes them, establishes their proportional fabric and constituent and comparative relationships, is monumentality.

What does the monumental order signify? It can be assumed that its first significance was the need for security during great historic crises; this was certainly the case in the decade 1929–1939, when all Europe became proudly nationalistic, and the USSR had to face considerable problems posed by the Revolution; under these conditions the conservative image of a monumental architecture could signify the strength of the institutions in the democracies, and equally the aggressive power of the State in the dictatorships.

In 1948, shortly after the end of the Second World War, the monumental order was introduced with a public debate in *The Architectural Review*[2] among the leading figures of the Modern Movement. They asked themselves three questions: What is monumentality? Is monumentality desirable today? How can monumentality be achieved? Then the concept of monumentality, after having been too long compressed into the creative image of contemporary architecture, began to break out and to propagate itself. It expressed a new need for security amid the crisis posed by the coexistence of the ideological system of the American 'Empire', and of a European society in a state of transition sometimes subordinate to American values and sometimes proudly attached to its own, while at the same time laboriously devoted to its quest for unity.

The memory of the Classical presents itself as deliverance and security, as a defence of human values in the face of attack from vulgar consumerism and the technological dynamics.

The monumental order ensures the declamatory quality of architecture, the need for rhetoric that can be identified with the symbolism of power. It invests, for example, the American skyscraper, redeeming it from being simply a pragmatic exploitation of the land and presenting it as an important symbol of its clientèle and of economic power – an architecture of pure idealism alongside the functional considerations that generated it. The American city thus becomes a cousin of Piranesi's *Field of Mars in Ancient Rome*.[3]

Today as in the 1930s, the monumental order provides a supernational language, a cultural language beyond all parochialism, every dialect and every vernacular. Today as in the 1930s, the monumental order suggests the marriage of ancient and modern according to a formula that involves not passive copying and repetition, but, in literary terms, allusion, sometimes even tongue-in-cheek. Quoting a text does not simply mean reproducing it, but reading it to some purpose, with a precise intent. It means making use of a text rather than simply serving it up. The quotation may be distorting in its apparent philologism, tendentious in its proclaimed objectivity. But the quotation belongs, like the memory, to the springs of identity, filtering the data of the reading as the memory filters the perception of reality; no memory is neutral, no quotation pure philology.

We are rendered impotent by rationalism and dogmatic formulas by which function must dictate form; we are surfeited by the economic exploitation of the International Style, saturated by the brutal colonialism that it represents in all the newly developing countries; the appearance of the monumental order, the essence of Classicism, stands not as a principle of authority according to the ancient model and therefore as an expression of obedience, but as a gesture of liberty. It is no accident that the monumental order triumphs when liberty is threatened.

NOTES

INTRODUCTION

1. 'Novecento' (or '1900') indicates primarily an Italian movement that had some influence throughout Europe. It originated in the field of the fine arts, then spread to architecture, the decorative arts and expressions of taste in general. In poetry and language it involved a return to realism (Picasso painted his *Portrait de femme avec son enfant* and *L'italienne* in this period), which assumed various aspects in literature, from Severini's 'idéiste' realism to Bontempelli's 'magique' realism, and explored, on the one hand, the conjunction between reality and tradition, valid for architecture too, and, on the other, an abstract, Surrealist vein associated with the avant-garde.

'EUPALINOS OU L'ARCHITECTE'

1. Paul Valéry, in a letter of 20 January 1934 to the Academy Inspector Dontenville. The letter is reproduced in the current editions of *Eupalinos*.
2. 'Tu ne saurais croire, Socrate, quelle joie c'était pour mon âme de connâtre une chose si bien réglée. Je ne sépare plus l'idée d'un temple de celle de son édification. En voyant un, je vois une action admirable, plus glorieuse encore qu'une victoire et plus contraire à la misérable nature.'
This and all subsequent quotations in this chapter are taken from *Eupalinos ou l'Architecte*, Paul Valéry, *Oeuvres Complètes*, Vol.II, Paris 1960.
3. 'progettare è pensare eseguibile'.
4. 'architecture parlante'.
5. 'l'avant-garde maudite'.

ARCHITECTURE AND REVOLUTION

ITALY

1. Karel Teige, *Arte e Ideologia*, Turin 1982, p.21.
2. Giovanni Giolitti, politician, several times Presidente del Consiglio (Prime Minister), personifies a period when the bourgeoisie's self-confidence, newly-acquired through the country's industrialisation, was accompanied by several tactful and clever social 'openings'. Fascism considered him its enemy number one and gave the nickname 'Italietta' to the Italy he had built up by cultivating good public administration, the nationalist, interventionist Italy, to which D'Annunzio and the Futurists had contributed the idea of a vital, 'avant-garde' dynamism.
3. Giuseppe Pagano Pogatsching, founder of *Casabella*, a nationalist who crossed over to the Resistance, and died at Mauthausen before the Liberation.
4. E. Ludwig, *Colloqui con Mussolini*, Milan 1932, p.203.
5. Roberto Farinacci, journalist and dignitary of the Fascist régime, extremist and sectarian, opposed to the position of Grandi and Bottai during the meeting of the Gran Consiglio on the night of 25 July 1943 which brought about the deposition of Mussolini, pro-Nazi, director of the Republic of Salo, executed by the partisans. He was practically the symbol of violent and rhetorical 'squadrismo', obstructing even Mussolini's prudent and artful 'transformism' in some cases when he was obliged to adapt to the exigencies of government, which he (Farinacci) opposed with constant reminders of the violent and 'revolutionary' origins of Fascism.
6. Giuseppe Bottai, Fascist director, founder of the 'corporations' of which he was undersecretary and Minister, Minister of National Education, Governor of Rome; in the debate within Fascism made himself spokesman for a tendency to make overtures to the opponents and the 'bigi' (greys), as those were called who were neither red Marxists nor black Fascists, after the colour of their famous shirts, the colour that predominated in their uniforms and in the régime's rituals. Bottai was the founder of two magazines, *Critica Fascista* and *Primato*, which opened a cultural debate and earned him the description 'critical Fascist'. Sided with Grandi on 25 July 1943, enrolled in the Foreign Legion and fought valiantly in the war of liberation, winning the rank of sergeant on the field under the pseudonym 'Sergeant Battle'.
7. G.A. Platz, *Die Baukunst der neusten Zeit*, Berlin 1930.

GERMANY

8. Fritz Todt, German engineer, responsible under the Nazi régime for the construction of motorways and later, during the war, of the Siegfried Line, Atlantic Wall, and Gothic Line fortifications. The Todt Organisation which was set up to deal with unemployment during the early years of Nazism, became an auxiliary of the Wehrmacht and exploited about 2 million deportees from occupied countries as labourers.
9. Elias Canetti, *Potere e Sopravvivenza*, Milan 1974, p.95.

RUSSIA

10. Karel Teige, *Arte e Ideologia*, Turin 1982, p.53.

NOTES

11. F. Taunus, in L. Patetta, *La monumentalità nell'architettura moderna*, Milan 1982, p.32.
12. G. Semper, *On architectonic style*, discourse in Zurich in 1869, reproduced in Patetta, *op. cit.*, p.88.
13. Joseph Roth, *Reise in Russland*, Cologne 1976, p.138.
14. Leon Trotsky, *Littérature et Révolution*, Paris 1967, p.209.
15. *Op. cit.*, p.219.
16. *Op. cit.*, p.264.
17. André Lurçat, 'Retour d'Union Soviétique', in *Art Vivant*, 1934, p.161.
18. *Op. cit.*
19. Quoted by B. Cassetti, 'André Lurçat in URSS', in *Socialismo, Città, Architettura, URSS 1917-1937*, Rome 1971, pp.208-209.
20. Quoted by B. Cassetti, *op. cit.*, p.214.
21. B. Cassetti, *op. cit.*, pp.214-215.
22. Anatole Kopp, *Ville et Révolution*, Paris 1967, p.225.
23. Quoted by Anatole Kopp, *op. cit.*, p.226.
24. M. Tzapenko, *Des bases réalistes de l'architecture soviétique*, Moscow 1952, quoted by Anatole Kopp.
25. Quoted by Anatole Kopp, *op. cit.*, p.236.

THE MONUMENTAL ORDER

1. Lewis Mumford in *The Architectural Review*, April 1949.
2. *Ibid.*
3. Faguswerk (Fagus factory), one of Gropius' best known buildings, considered to be a manifesto of the Modern Movement, uses subtly optical corrections and complete entasis of the straight pillars at the front, which links the work to the Vitruvian 'temperaturae' tradition and the aesthetics of proportion, widely cultivated in the nineteenth century by Choisy and Thiersch.
4. Hans Poelzig, *Gesammelte Schriften und Werke*, Berlin 1970.
5. Pierre Francastel, *Art et technique*, Paris 1956.
6. 'Terranova' rough-cast, a plaster coloured in the body, boasted some vivid shades such as an ochre more like egg-yolk, and a red supposed to derive from Pompeii but reminiscent of anti-rust cinnabar paint. At Pistoia people gave the nickname 'yellow palace' to their only Novecento building of the period, the work of Raffaello Brizzi.
7. Hugo Häring, *Das andere Bauen*, Stuttgart 1982.
8. Hugo Häring, *ibid.*

NATIONAL SPIRIT

ENGLAND

1. D. Dean, *The Thirties: recalling the English architectural scene*, London 1983, p.14.
2. C. and T. Benton, *Architecture: contrasts of a decade* in Exhibition Catalogue *The Thirties*, Hayward Gallery, London 1979.

GERMANY

3. The Zehner Ring was a group of ten architects (subsequently twenty-five) founded by Taut between 1923 and 1924, to which belonged Scharoun, Mies van der Rohe, Poelzig, Mendelsohn, Hilbersheimer, Behrendt, the brothers Bruno and Max Taut, Bartning, Häring, and later the brothers Luckhardt, Körn, Döcker, Meyer, Gropius, Hasler, May, Rading, Lauterbach, Schneider, Soeder, Behrens, Tessenow and the Viennese Frank and Hoffmann. Häring was the Ring's secretary, and represented them at the 1928 CIAM congress in Switzerland.
4. Hans Poelzig, *L'architetto*, 1931, in *Scritti e Opere*, *op. cit.*, Ch.4, p.290.
5. Hans Poelzig, *ibid.*
6. Hans Poelzig, *ibid.*

ITALY

7. Roberto Papini, 'Architettura e decorazione', in *Le arti a Monza nel MCMXXII*, Bergamo 1923, quoted by L. Patetta, *L'architettura in Italia 1919-1922*, Milan 1972, p.67.
8. Roberto Papini, 'Architetti giovani in Roma', in *Dedalo*, 1932, quoted by L. Patetta, *op. cit.*, p.99.
9. Gruppo 7, 'Architettura e una renova epoca arcaica', in *La Rassegna Italiana*, 1926-7, quoted by L. Patetta, *op. cit.*, p.120.
10. C.E. Rava, 'Svolta pericolosa (Situazione dell'Italia di fronte al razionalismo europeo)' in *Domus*, Jan-Nov 1931, quoted by L. Patetta, *op. cit.*, pp.171-172.
11. In 1931, the year when Fascism paid most attention to architecture, and when the city plan for Rome was approved which affected the city's fate even after the war, the modernist or 'Novecentisti' architects applied to take part in the construction of the 'great works of the régime'. The latter development was intended to limit the ravages of the 1929 economic crisis, which affected Italy slightly less than some countries, but still severely.
12. *Manifesto per l'architettura razionale*, reproduced in Patetta, *op. cit.*, p.192.

NOTES

13. Giuseppe Belli, popular nineteenth-century Roman poet.

14. Plinio Marconi, 'Architettura italiana attuale', in *Architettura*, special number for the Milan Triennale 1933, quoted by L. Patetta, *op. cit.*, pp.243–244.

15. M. Piacentini, 'Difesa dell'architettura italiana', in *Il Giornale d'Italia* of 2 May 1931, quoted by L. Patetta, *op. cit.*, p.299.

16. M. Piacentini, *ibid.*

17. 'Squadrismo' from 'squadre d'azione' (action squads) – groups of Blackshirts who, during the period 1919–22, carried out so-called 'punitive' expeditions against representatives of the democratic parties or simple, peace-loving anti-Fascists, who were usually attacked by groups of 'manganellatori' (cudgellers) or 'warned' by means of a stiff dose of castor oil.

18. M. Bontempelli, 'L'architettura come morale e politica', in *L'avventura novecentista*, Florence 1938, p.477.

BELGIUM

19. R.L. Delevoy, L.M. De Koninck, Exhibition Catalogue *London, Brussels*, 1973, pp.22–23.

20. Les Archives d'Architecture moderne, 14, rue Defacqz, Brussels, is an institution that performs the valuable work of collecting drawings and documents about nineteenth- and twentieth-century Belgian art. It also publishes a journal, *AAM*, and an ongoing series of monographs. Directed by M. Culot, it avails itself of a group of experts, notable among whom is Annick Brauman.

HOLLAND

21. G. Fanelli, *Architettura moderna in Olanda*, Florence 1968, p.108.

22. G. Fanelli, *Architettura edilizia urbanistica, Olanda 1917–1940*, Florence 1978, which amplifies the previous highly successful book.

23. G. Fanelli, *op. cit.*, p.471.

24. G. Fanelli, *op. cit.*, p.482.

25. G. Fanelli, *op. cit.*, p.534.

26. G. Fanelli, *op. cit.*, p.549.

27. G. Fanelli, *op. cit.*, pp.560–561.

28. G. Fanelli, *op. cit.*, p.561.

29. J.J.P. Oud, 'Riesamina se stesso', in *Metron* No.45, 1952, pp.9–10.

30. J.J.P. Oud, *op. cit.*, p.8.

31. J.J.P. Oud, *op. cit.*, p.9.

32. J.J.P. Oud, *op. cit.*, p.12.

33. J.J.P. Oud, *op. cit.*, p.14.

34. J.J.P. Oud, *op. cit.*, p.14.

SCANDINAVIA

35. *Nordic Classicism*, Museum of Finnish Architects, Helsinki 1982.

36. A. Milelli, 'E.G. Asplund', in *Controspazio* No.4, 1983, p.15.

37. D. Porphyrius, 'Scandinavia and Doricism', in *Architectural Design*, May–June 1982, pp.23–25.

FRANCE

38. M. Raynaud, D. Laroque, S. Rémy, *Roux-Spitz*, Liège 1983.

39. M.L. Biver, *Le Paris de Napoléon*, Paris 1963, the chapter 'Le palais du Roi de Rome sur la montagne de Chaillot', pp.326ff.

40. A. Whittick, *European Architecture of the Twentieth Century*, London 1950–3, new edition Aylesbury 1974.
E.H. Rogers, *Auguste Perret*, Milan 1955.
P. Collins, *Concrete. The Vision of the new Architecture*, London 1969.

41. R. Banham, *Theory and Design in the First Machine Age*, London 1960.

42. F. Laisney, in *R.H. Expert*, Paris 1983, p.121.

43. Alain, *Système des beaux-arts*, Paris 1926, p.186.

44. Alain, *op. cit.*, pp.186–188.

45. Alain, *op. cit.*, p.190.

46. Alain, *op. cit.*, p.190.

47. R. Gabelli and C. Olmo, *Le Corbusier et 'l'Esprit Nouveau'*, Turin 1975, pp.50–51.

48. *Ibid.*

49. *Ibid.*

50. *Ibid.*

51. Le Corbusier, *Vers une architecture*, Paris 1924, p.79.

MATERIALS

1. Galuchat is sharkskin, used for its prized texture and colour to upholster furniture in both Art Deco and 1930s styles.

CONCLUSION: PERSPECTIVES

1. John Summerson, *The Classical Language of Architecture*, London 1963.

2. The debate was published in *The Architectural Review* of September 1948, and Lewis Mumford's contribution in April 1949.

3. The panels of *Il Campo Marzio dell'Antica Roma* by G.B. Piranesi (Rome 1762) offer an imaginative reproduction of the 'city of *ludus*' contained between the Capitol, Via Lata and the Tiber as far as the Colles Hortulorum, through plans that cover a casual assembly and an interpretation of late Imperial Roman architecture from Borromini to Ledoux.

SELECTED BIBLIOGRAPHY

The period of the 1930s and the particular style which is the subject of this book are covered in most general works on modern architecture. One can refer, therefore, to the works by Bruno Zevi, L. Benevolo, Kenneth Frampton, Ragon, Henry-Russell Hitchcock, and Arnold Whittick, among others. A specific evaluation of the style does not exist and it is best to refer to articles in the specialist journals of the time. These include: for France, *L'Architecture, La Construction moderne, Architecture d'aujourd'hui, Art et Décoration*; for Britain, *The Architectural Review*; for Germany, *Moderne Bauformen* and *Innendekoration*; for Italy, *Domus* and *Casabella*. To this list can be added the ideas expounded in *Le Système des beaux-arts* by Alain (Paris 1926) and above all by *Eupalinos ou l'architecte* by Valéry, reprinted in his complete works (volume II, Paris 1960). Equally essential is *Vers une architecture* by Le Corbusier (Paris 1924), translated as *Towards a new architecture* (London 1927).

The list of works on the architecture of particular countries is far from being exhaustive. We have simply selected a few basic studies which have the same sort of approach as this book.

For the Soviet Union: Cohen J.L., De Michelis M. and Tafuri M.: *URSS 1917–1978. La Ville, l'architecture*, Rome and Paris 1979; Kopp A.: *Ville et Révolution*, Paris 1967; *L'Architecture de la période stalinienne*, Grenoble and Paris 1978.

For Germany and Austria, among works generally available: Häring H.: *Il segreto della forma*, Milan 1983; Pentsch J.: *Baukunst und Stadtplanung im Dritten Reich*, Munich 1976; Platz G.A.: *Die Baukunst der neusten Zeit*, Berlin 1930; Sembach K.J.: *Stil 1930*, Tübingen 1984; Taut A.: *Architektur im Dritten Reich*, Berlin 1977.
Among monographs: Heuss T.: *Hans Poelzig, das Lebenbild eines deutschen Baumeisters*, Berlin 1939; Poelzig H.: *Gesammelte Schriften und Werke*, Berlin 1970; Larsson L.O.: *Albert Speer, Le plan de Berlin 1937–1943*, Brussels 1982; Krier L.: *Albert Speer*, Brussels 1985; Wangerin G. and Weiss G.: *Heinrich Tessenow*, Essen 1976; Sekler E.F.: *Joseph Hoffmann*, Vienna 1982.

For Britain: 'Britain in the Thirties', *Architectural Design*, special issue, profile 24; Dean D.: *The Thirties: Recalling the English Architectural Scene*, London 1983, and *Architecture of the 1930s*, New York 1983; Farr D.: *English Art 1870–1940*, Oxford 1978; Gould J.: *Modern Houses in Britain, 1919–1939*, London 1979; Inskip P.: *E. Lutyens*, London 1979; Pevsner N.: 'Gordon Russell', in *Studies in Art, Architecture and Design*, Scarborough 1968, vol.II, pp.211f.; *Thirties: British Art and Design before the War*, exhibition catalogue, Arts Council, 1979.

For Italy, among general works: Patetta L.: *L'architettura in Italia. Le polemiche*, Milan 1972; Patetta L.: *La monumentalità nell'architettura moderna*, Turin 1982, and *L'architettura in Italia 1919–1943*, Milan 1972; Bottai G.: *Politica fascista delle arti*, Rome 1940; Piacentini M.: *Architettura d'oggi*, Rome 1930; Piacentini M.: 'Gli archi e le colonne e la modernità d'oggi' in *La Tribuna*, 21 February 1933; Borsi F. et al.: *Il Palazzo dell'Industria*, Rome 1986; Mazzochi G. et al.: *27/78 Architettura*, Milan 1979; Giovannoni G.: *Vecchie città e edilizia nuova*, Turin 1931; Persico E.: *Scritti critici e polemici*, Milan 1947; Persico E.: *Scritti d'architettura. 1927–35*, Florence 1968; De Finetti G.: *Milano costruzione di una città*, Milan 1969; De Seta C.: *La cultura architettonica in Italia tra le due guerre*, Bari 1972; Giolli R.: *L'architettura razionale*, Bari 1972; Valeriani E.: *Del Debbio*, Rome 1976; Pozzetto M.: *Aloisio*, Turin 1977; Portoghesi P., Massobrio G.: *Album degli Anni '30*, Bari 1978; Gambisario G., Minardi B.: *Giovanni Muzio. Opere e scritti*, Milan 1982. *Anni Trenta, Architettura a Firenze*, exhibition catalogue, Casa di Dante, Florence 1984; Pasquali G., Pinna P.: *Sabaudia 1933–34*, Milan 1985.
Among monographs: Zevi B.: *Giuseppe Terragni*, Bologna 1980; Portoghesi P. and Pansera A.: *Gio Ponti alla manifattura di Doccia*, Milan 1982; Piacentini M.: *Curriculum vitae di Marcello Piacentini*, Rome 1955; Riccesi D.: *Gustavo Pulitzer Finali, il disegno della nave*, Venice 1985; *Pietro Aschieri architetto*, special number, Bollettino Biblioteca Facoltà di Architettura di Roma, Rome 1977; *Angiolo Mazzoni, architetto nell'Italia fra le due guerre*, exhibition catalogue, Galleria Comunale d'arte moderna, Bologna 1984–85.

For Belgium, the most important works are those from the Archives d'Architecture moderne: Strauven F.: *René Braem*, Brussels 1985; Delevoy R.L.: *Antoine Pompe*, Brussels 1974; Delevoy R.L. and Culot M.: *De Koninck*, Brussels 1980. See also: Borsi F. and Portoghesi P.: *Victor Horta*, Brussels 1977.

For the Netherlands, among general works: Fanelli G.: *Architettura moderna in Olanda*, Florence 1968, and *Architettura edilizia urbanistica, Olanda 1917/1940*, Florence 1978; *Moderne Bouwkunst in Nederland* (a series of 12 small volumes on Dutch architecture between the wars), Rotterdam 1932-1936; Sharp D.: 'Progress and Tradition in Modern Dutch Architecture', in *RIBA Journal*, March 1965, pp.136-141; *Amsterdam 1920-1960*, exhibition catalogue, Stedelijk Museum, Amsterdam 1983.
Among monographs: Stamm G.: *J.J.P. Oud, Bauten und Projekte 1906 bis 1963*, Mainz 1984; Cramer M. et al.: *W.M. Dudok 1884-1974*, Amsterdam 1980.

For Scandinavia, general works include: Rasmussen S.E.: *Nordische Baukunst*, Berlin 1940; Kidder-Smith G.E.: *Sweden Builds*, New York and Stockholm 1950; *Nordic Classicism, 1910-1930*, exhibition catalogue, Museum of Finnish Architecture, Helsinki 1982; *The Classical Tradition and the Modern Movement*, 2nd International Alvar Aalto Symposium, Helsinki 1985. Among monographs, it is worth noting the recent work on *Asplund* by C. Caldenby and O. Hultin, Stockholm 1985.

Finally, in the case of France, there are few general works on the period. We can mention the excellent *Retour à l'ordre dans les arts plastiques et l'architecture, 1919-1925* published by the University of Saint-Étienne (1986). Another interesting work from a university is: *Le Jeu des modèles, les modèles en jeu*, by J.-Cl. Vigato, school of architecture, Nancy, CEMPA, 1980. The period of the 1930s is well covered in *l'Histoire de l'architecture moderne en France*, by René Jullian, Paris 1984. See also: Malkiel Jirmounsky M.: *Les tendances de l'architecture contemporaine*, Paris 1930; *Les Réalismes*, exhibition catalogue, Centre Pompidou, Paris 1981.

For monographs on designers and furniture-makers, one should study the works from Éditions du Regard: Chanaux A.: *Jean-Michel Frank*, Paris 1980; Camard F.: *Ruhlmann*, Paris 1983; Vellay M. and Frampton K.: *Pierre Chareau*, Paris 1984; Bujon G.: *Eugène Printz*, Paris 1985; also interesting: Rubino L.: *Pierre Chareau e Bernard Bijvoet*, Rome 1982.

Works on architects: Van Moos C.: *Le Corbusier, l'architecte et son mythe*, Paris 1970; *Roger Henri-Expert*, collected works published by IFA, with contributions by M. Culot, F. Loyer, H. Guéné et al., Paris 1983; Deshoulières D. and Jeanneau H.: *Rob. Mallet-Stevens*, Brussels 1980; Pinchon J.-F.: *Edouard et Jean Niermans*, Liège 1985; Rogers E.M.: *Auguste Perret*, Milan 1955; Raynaud M., Laroque D. and Rémy S.: *Roux-Spitz*, Liège 1983; Sarazin C.: *Henri Sauvage*, Brussels 1978; *Paul Tournon*, collected works, Paris 1976; Gournay I.: *Le nouveau Trocadéro*, Brussels 1985.

THE MONUMENTAL ERA

LIST OF ILLUSTRATIONS

AUSTRIA

- Pavilion at the Venice Biennale, 1934, 104, 109.
- Pavilion at the Paris International Exhibition, 1937, 172.

BELGIUM

- Brussels: Royal Albertine Library, 50, 119. Métropole Cinema, 83. Gare centrale, 122. Gare du midi, 123. Motorway intersection, 195.
- Liège: German house at the International Water Exhibition, 1932, 109.
- Wygmael: Rémy factory, 1930, 120.
- Ghent: University library tower, 120.

ENGLAND

- London: RIBA building, 19, 95. Reuters news agency, 90. Battersea Power Station, 101. London University, 102.
- Cambridge: University Library, 86.
- Sheffield: City Hall, 98.
- War memorials in France, 53.
- House, 98.

FINLAND

- Helsinki: Parliament building, 138.

FRANCE

- Paris International Exhibition, 1937: 170, 171, 172, 173. German pavilion, 33. Austrian pavilion, 172. Italian pavilion, 110, 172. Jugoslav pavilion, 96–97. Railway pavilion, 141. Metal pavilion, 156. Pavillon des Artistes décorateurs, 156. About pavilion, 156.
- Paris Colonial Exhibition, 1931: 166, 167. Musée des colonies, 14, 15, 174. Fountains, 148–149.
- Design for the layout of the Porte Maillot, 48–49, 50.
- Musée des Travaux publics, 56, 57, 61.
- Mobilier national, 59.
- Church of the Saint-Esprit, 63.
- Church in Elisabethville, 69.
- Church of St Theresa in Montmagny, 66.
- Fire-station at Passy, 75.
- Church of St Nicholas (design), 76.
- Town-hall at Boulogne-Billancourt, 85, 145.
- Design for the OUTA, Paris, 91.
- Terrace of the Bestégui apartment, 140.
- Building in Place Vauban, 78–79.
- Palais de Chaillot, 14, 141.
- Musée de la Ville de Paris, 142.
- Annexe for the Bibliothèque Nationale at Versailles, 146.
- Apartment in the Rue Litolff, 147.
- Perret office, 158.
- Bély store, 158.
- Carmaud: St Benedict's Church, 71.
- Dinard: villa by Roux-Spitz, 147.
- Liner *Normandie*: 150, 151.
- Decorative arts: ironwork, 156, 158, 159. Furniture, 153, 176, 177, 178, 179. Glass, 183, 185. Jewellery, 160, 161, 165. Bindings, 157. Lighting, 162, 163. Prints, 190, 191. Designs for jewellery, 188, 189.
- Materials: ceramics, 187. Earthenware, 186, 187. Lacquer, 186, 187. Galuchat, 180. Gypsum, 180.

GERMANY

- Hanover: Stadthalle, 29.
- Munich: Kunsthaus, 30. Ehrentempel, 30.
- Cologne: Church of St Elisabeth, 66–67.
- Nuremberg: Zeppelin field, 30.
- Berlin: Ober-Kommando der Wehrmacht, 31. Grosse Halle, 31. Reichshauptbank, 88. Süd-Bahnhof, 93. Rhenania Haus, 105, Olympic stadium, 158. Design for the Schauburg, 106. Design for the national memorial, 106. Soldatenhalle, 67.
- Hindenburg: Church of St Joseph, 66.
- Essen: Church of St Engelbert, 72.
- Dulmen: Church of the Holy Cross, 73.
- Frankfurt: I G Farben offices, 107.

ITALY

- Florence: station, 25.
- Rome: Headquarters of the Ente Nazionale per Mutilati e Invalidi di Guerra, 26. University City, 26. Design for Auditorium, 113. Design for Palazzo della Civiltà Italiana, 114.
- Bolzano: Victory monument, 26.
- Milan: Restructuring of Arena district, 51. Rasini tower, 81. Building in Piazza Duse, 81, 116. Building in Via Melzi d'Eril, 81. Building in Piazza Cinque Giornate, 81. Design for reconstruction of city centre, 15. Trade Union Building, 116. Palazzo dell'Arte, 117. Palazzo Fidia, 117. Building on the Via Giorgio Jan, 117. Building on the Via Serbelloni, 117. Design for building of Il Popolo d'Italia, 114.
- Turin: Design for Via Roma, 77.

JUGOSLAVIA

- French Embassy in Belgrade, 143.
- Pavilion at the Paris International Exhibition, 1937, 96, 97.

NETHERLANDS

- Hilversum: Town Hall, 126.
- Blijdorps: Zoo, 127.
- The Hague: Shell Building, 128, 129.

SWEDEN

- Stockholm: Concert Hall, 133. Crematorium, 135. Public Library, 136.
- Gothenburg: Town Hall extension, 134.

USSR

- Moscow: Narkomtiajprom building, 14, 15. Apartment blocks, 84, 85. Residential block 'on the Moskovaia', 46. Design for the Palace of the Soviets, 42, 43, 44, 45. Administrative building, 46. Underground station, 38. Design for the Academy of Sciences, 40. Rostov Theatre, 85. Armenian pavilion at the Agricultural Economy Exhibition, 1938, 168. Design for People's Commissariat for Heavy Industry, 38.

OUTSIDE EUROPE

- Cathedral at Casablanca, 11.
- Design for Royal Palace in Baghdad, 168.
- Maison du Colon in Mascara, Algeria, 169.
- Design for the Town Hall in Algiers, 169.
- State Bank in Casablanca, 169.

INDEX

Page references in italic refer to captions for illustrations appearing on those pages; other references are to the text.

Aalto, Alvar 138
Alabian, K. *168*
Alain 13, 145, 152, 154
Andoiantz, A. *46*
Andreani, Aldo *117*
Art Deco 10, 54, 55, 118, 152, 154, 157, 159, 164, 175, 193
Art Nouveau 9, 10, 13, 54, 55, 83, 99, 118, 154, 159, 164, 175, 181
Aschieri, Pietro 115
Asplund, Erik-Gunnar 132, *134, 135, 136, 137*

Badovici, Jean 20
Banham, Reyner 143
Barovieroso 184
Bassompierre 77
Baudry, Léon *151*
Bauhaus 39, 104, 124
Bayet, J. 20
Behrens, Peter 27, 29, 54, 100
Berlage, H.P. 124
Bitherlin *158*
Blomfield, Sir Reginald 99
Blomme, Adrien *83, 123*
Blomme, Y. *123*
Boeken 125
Bofil, Ricardo 195
Böhm, Dominikus 27, 66, 67, 68, *72, 73,* 107
Boileau, Louis Auguste 139
Bonatz, Paul 28, *29,* 68, 107
Bonnet, Paul *157*
Bontempelli, M. 114
Bordoni, Antonio *116*
Borissavlievitch 87
Bottai, Giuseppe 24
Boulée, Etienne Louis 132, 137
Bourgeois, Victor 27, 80, 118
Braem, René 118, *119,* 121, *192*
Brasini, Armando *167*
Brecker, Arno *67*
Brunfault, G. *50,* 121
Butterfield, William 99

Canetti, Elias 28, 32
Caneva, L.M. *116*
Carlu, Jacques 139
Carminati, Antonio *116*
Chambon, Alfred *195*
Chappey, Marcel *91*
Chareau, Pierre 164, 182
Chermayeff, Serge 99
Chiesa, Pietro 184
Chirico, Giorgio de 48

Choisy, Auguste 20, 143
CIAM 39, 94, 124
Coco Chanel 12
Cocteau, Jean 10, 12
Collins, P. 142, 143
Coulon, A. *185*
Croce, Benedetto 13, 145
Cubism 74, 76, 125
Cuzzi, Umberto 77, *194*
Czeschka 108

Daum *183*
Debat-Ponsan, J.H.E. *82*
De Koninck, L.M. 118
Delaunay, Robert *141,* 170
Delevoy, R.L. 118
Deligne, J. *120,* 121
Desprès, J. *160, 161, 165, 189*
De Stijl 81, 82, 124, 159
Drivier *142*
Duchamp-Villon, G. 76
Dudok, W.-M. 99, 100, *126*
Dufrène, Maurice *155, 162*
Dufy, Raoul 170, *186, 187*
Duiker, Johannes 27

Eisenman, Peter 195
Expert, R.-H. 143, *143,* 144, *148, 149*
Expressionism 27, 74, 99, 107

Fahrenkamp, Emil 27, 68, *105,* 107, 108, *109,* 112
Fanelli, G. 124
Farinacci, Roberto 24
Fasolo 115
Fischer, Theodor 87
Finetti, G. *15, 51, 92*
Fischer, Theodor 87
Fomin, Ivan A. 38
Foschini, Arnaldo 115
Francastel, Pierre 74
Frank, J.-M. 108, 164, *176, 179, 180*
Frizia, Elio *81*
Fry, Maxwell 99

Garcia, Artita *157*
Garnier, Tony 62, *85,* 139, 144, *145*
Gelfreikh, V. *35, 42, 85*
Giolitti, Giovanni 23
Gori, Georges *110*
Goulden, Jean *186*
Grassi, Georgio 195
Gromort 144
Gropius, Walter 27, 60, 99, 112, 126, 130, 131, 195
Guadet, Julien 143
Guénot *142*
Guermanovitch, S. *44*

Hagen, G. 107
Häring, Hugo 87

Harris, E.V. *98*
Harvey, J.D.M. *19*
Hawksmoor, Nicholas 99
Hertlein 107
Hill, Oliver 99
Hitler, Adolf 9, 12, 18, 23, 28, 29, 32, 33, 35, 36, 112
Hoffmann, Josef 55, *104*, 108, *109*, 144, 181, 182
Holden, Charles *102*
Holliday, Theodore *101*
Holzmeister, Clemens 108, 166, *168*
Horta, Victor 10, 82, 118, 121, *122*
Hoste, Huib 118, 121
Huet-Tchumy-Vermeil *151*

Issel 69, 107
Ivacci, I. *96, 97*

Janniot *142*
Jaussely, Léon *14, 15, 166*
Jeannot *153*
Johansson, Cyrillus 137
Johnson, Philip 195
Joltovsky, I. *45, 46*
Joubov, A. *43*
Jourdain, Francis 164

Kahn, Louis 195
Kampmann, Hack 137
Kieffer, Michel *157*
Kleihues, Josef 195
Kreis, Wilhelm 27, *67*
Krejcar, Jaromir 39
Krier, R. and L. 195

Lancia, Emilio 27, 60, *81*, 115
La Padula, Ernesto 62
Laprade, Albert *14, 15, 166*
Le Corbusier 10, 18, 20, 21, 22, 37, 41, 55, 87, 88, 99, 118, 121, 125, 126, 127, 132, 139, *140*, 144, 152, 154, 157, 164, 184, 193
Ledoux, Claude Nicolas 132, 137
Lemaitre *174*
Lewerentz, Sigurd 137
L'Herbier, M. 143
Libera, A. 24, *113*, 115
Liebermann, Max 108
Linazasoro, José Ignazio 195
Lipchitz, J. 164
Lissitsky, El 125
Loquet 121
Lubetkin, Berthold 99
Ludwig, E. 23
Lukacs 37
Lurçat, André 39, 40, *40*, 41, 139
Lutyens, Sir Edwin *53*, 90, *90*, 99, 166
Lyautey, Marshal 166

Mallet-Stevens, Robert 74, 75, 76, 87, 140, 143
March, Werner *158*
Marconi, Plinio 112
Marinot *183*
Markelius, Sven 137
May, Ernst 39
Mayakovsky 37, 47
Melnikov, K.S. *14*
Mendelsohn, Eric 99, 100, 112
Mere, Clement *177, 179*
Meyer, Hannes 39
Miller, Carl *133*
Molière, G. 125
Mondrian, Piet 82
Moretti, L. *114*, 115
Moser, Karl 68
Mussolini, Benito 12, 22, 23, 24, 25, 60, 111, 112
Muzio, Giovanni 60, 62, *114*, 115, *117*

Neutra, Richard 130
Nicolas, Raymond 83
Niermans, E. and J. *169*
Normandie 143, 144, *150, 151*
Novecento 9, 10, 24, 27, 40, 52, 74
Novello, Alberto *81*

Ojetti 112
Östberg, Ragnar 137
Oud, J.J.P. 126, 127, *128, 129*, 130, 131, 195

Pagano, Giuseppe 23, 24
Palladio, Andrea 99
Papini, Roberto 111
Paris, Gaston *173*
Pei, I.M. 195
Perret, Auguste *14*, *27*, *56, 58, 59, 60, 61*, 68, *70, 71, 72, 73*, 142, 143, *158*
Piacentini, Marcello 24, 25, *26*, 27, 60, 112
Platz, G.A. 27
Poelzig, Hans 27, 64, *64*, *65*, 68, *88, 89*, *106*, 107, *107*, 108
Pommier, Robert *78*
Ponti, Gio 18, 27, 60, *81*, 115, *187*
Portallupi, Piero 115, *117*
Posokin, M. *46*
Pulitzer 27
Purini, Franco 195

Ramekers, J. 121
Rasmussen, Steen Eiler 137
Rava, Carlo 111
Ridolfi, Mario 115
Rogers, E.H. 142
Rossi, Aldo 195
Roth, J. 36
Roux-Spitz, Michel 74, 139, 144, *146, 147*
Ruhlmann, J.E. *153*, 164, *176, 178*

Saenredam 124
Sarfatti, Margherita 24, 25
Sarrabezolles, Carlo *141, 143*
Sauvage, Henri 27, *48, 50*
Schinkel, Karl Friedrich 29, 137
Schtiouko, V. *35, 42, 85*
Schtoussev, A. *92*
Schumacher, Fritz 107
Schweizer, O.E. 107
Scott, Sir Giles Gilbert *86, 98,* 100, *101*
Semper, Gottfried 35
Shaw, Norman 99
Simonet, Albert *163*
Sirén, Johan Sigfrid *136, 138*
Smolin, D. *43*
Sofarian, S. *168*
Sottsass, E. *77*
Speer, Albert 28, *30, 31, 32, 33,* 34, *48,*
93
Staal, Arthur 124, 125
Stalin, Joseph 23, 39, 41, 47
Stam, Mart 39
Stone, Edward 195
Stravinsky, Igor 12
Subes, Raymond *151, 156, 158, 159*
Süe 20
Summerson, Sir John 195

Tatlin, Vladimir 39
Taut, Bruno 74, 104
Tchechoulin, P. *43*
Tchouka, A. *43*
Teige, Karel 22, 23
Templier, Raymond *186, 187*
Terragni, Giuseppe 24
Tessenow, Heinrich 28
Tessin, Nicodemus 132, 137

Todt, Fritz 28
Toscano, Gruppo *25*
Tournon, Paul *11,* 63, 69, *91*
Troost, P.L. 28, *30,* 48
Trotsky, Leon 37
Tzara, Tristan 12

Ulrich 115
Ungers, O.M. 195

Vaccaro, Domenico 24
Vaillat 20
Valéry, Paul 12, 16, *17,* 18, 20, 21, 91,
139, 142
Vanbrugh, John 99
Van Cleef et Arpels *188, 189*
Van der Rohe, Mies 29, 126, 127, 130,
195
Van de Velde, Henry *120,* 121
Van Loghem 39
Van Ravesteyn, Sybold 125, *127*
Van Woerden 125
Venini 184
Vichinsky, L. *45*
Vlasov, A. *44*

Wagner, Otto 48
Webb, Philip 99
Whittick, A. 142
Wittgenstein, L. 16, 82, 91
Wornum, Grey *19, 95,* 100
Wren, Sir Christopher 99
Wright, Frank Lloyd 130, 131

Yofan, B. *35, 42, 84*

Zanini, Gigiotti *81, 116*
Zevi, Bruno 131